STEPPING OUT INTO A GOOD LIFE WITH DEMENTIA

ONWARDS AND UPWARDS

JOE ASHTON

authorHOUSE

AuthorHouse™ UK
1663 Liberty Drive
Bloomington, IN 47403 USA
www.authorhouse.co.uk
Phone: 0800 047 8203 (Domestic TFN)
*　　　+44 1908 723714 (International)*

© 2020 Joe Ashton. All rights reserved.

No part of this book may be reproduced, stored in a retrieval system, or transmitted by any means without the written permission of the author.

Published by AuthorHouse 02/24/2020

ISBN: 978-1-7283-9872-3 (sc)
ISBN: 978-1-7283-9871-6 (e)

Print information available on the last page.

Any people depicted in stock imagery provided by Getty Images are models, and such images are being used for illustrative purposes only.
Certain stock imagery © Getty Images.

This book is printed on acid-free paper.

Because of the dynamic nature of the Internet, any web addresses or links contained in this book may have changed since publication and may no longer be valid. The views expressed in this work are solely those of the author and do not necessarily reflect the views of the publisher, and the publisher hereby disclaims any responsibility for them.

POEMS BY THE AUTHOR
CONTENTS

About the author xiii
Foreword to Book by Joe Sydney Ashton xvi

Monday, 4 July 2011 - A GOOD LIFE WITH DEMENTIA 1
Tuesday, 5 July 2011 - WHY AM I SHARING THE
    DEMENTIA JOURNEY? 2
Wednesday, 6 July 2011 - DOES EXCERCISE HELP? 3
Thursday, 7 July 2011 - THE BENEFITS OF EXCERCISE CONT 5
Friday, 8 July 2011 - ISSUES REGARDING COMMUNICATION 7
Saturday, 9 July 2011 - COMMUNICATION CONT 9
Monday, 11 July 2011 - SECLUSION V ISOLATION 10
Tuesday, 12 July 2011 - MAKING THE MOST OF THE NOW 11
Thursday, 21 July 2011 - WE DO NOT HAVE TO RELY ON
    MEMORY TO ENJOY TODAY 13
Wednesday, 3 August 2011 - LINKING THE PAST WITH TODAY 15
Tuesday, 9 August 2011 - NO, ONE FITS ALL SOLOUTION,
    IN DEMENTIA 17
Wednesday, 10 August 2011 - TIME LOST - TIME GAINED 18
Sunday, 21 August 2011 - THREATS - PERCEIVED OR
    OTHERWISE 20
Friday, 26 August 2011 - A TRUSTED, PROFESSIONAL EAR
    CAN ASSIST 21
Monday, 29 August 2011 - VALUABLE v VIABLE 23
Tuesday, 30 August 2011 - TODAY'S OPPORTUNITIES V
    THE REDUCTION IN YESTERDAY'S ABILITIES 24
Thursday, 1 September 2011 - HUMOUR CAN BE A MASSIVE
    SUPPORT 26
Friday, 9 September 2011 - PATIENT INVOLVEMENT IN
    EDUCATING HEALTH PROFESSIONALS 28
Saturday, 10 September 2011 - INTERTWINING THE PAST
    WITH THE PRESENT 30
Tuesday, 27 September 2011 - DONT FIGHT THE JOY OF PEACE 31

Friday, 7 October 2011 - APOLOGISING FOR PAIN CAUSED 33
Tuesday, 18 October 2011 - "I WAS GOING TO MAKE YOU
     REMEMBER IT!" 35
Thursday, 20 October 2011 - TRUST IN OTHERS
     UNDERSTANDING 37
Friday, 21 October 2011 - CARING FOR YOUR CARER 38
Tuesday, 25 October 2011 - KEEPING A POSITIVE OUTLOOK 40
Saturday, 29 October 2011 - A GOOD WEEK 42
Sunday, 30 October 2011 - ADAPTABILITY HELPS 43
Wednesday, 2 November 2011 - PEOPLE WITH DEMENTIA
     ARE NORMAL 44
Friday, 4 November 2011 - A SMALL TRIUMPH MEANS A LOT 45
Saturday, 5 November 2011 - ENJOY THE COMPANY OF
     THOSE WHOSE COMPANY YOU ENJOY 46
Sunday, 6 November 2011 - TRYING TO AVOID THOSE
     WHO BRING THE WORST OUT IN YOU 48
Monday, 7 November 2011 - CARER TRUST 50
Wednesday, 9 November 2011 - HELPING YOUR CARER NOT
     TO WORRY 52
Friday, 11 November 2011 - UNFORSEEN BENEFITS OF
     SHUTTING DOWN 54
Monday, 14 November 2011 - A SILENT FRIEND 55
Wednesday, 16 November 2011 - RESPECT 56
Sunday, 20 November 2011 - FOG THE LEVELLER 58
Tuesday, 22 November 2011 - A TRICKY WINDY PATH 60
Thursday, 24 November 2011 - TAKE THE RISK - HAVE
     YOUR VOICE HEARD 61
Monday, 28 November 2011 - A HELPFUL TECHNIQUE 62
Tuesday, 6 December 2011 - EMOTIONAL DIMENSIONS 63
Sunday, 11 December 2011 - KEEP IT SIMPLE 65
Friday, 16 December 2011 - REPORT ON DEMENTIA CARE
     IN ACUTE HOSPITAL WARDS 66
Wednesday, 21 December 2011 - MEMORIES 67
Wednesday, 28 December 2011 - THOUGHTS AS THE NEW
     YEAR APPROACHES 68
Friday, 30 December 2011 - EXPRESSING YOUR THOUGHTS
     and SEEKING CLARIFICATION 70
Friday, 3 February 2012 - UNCERTAIN TIMES 72

Wednesday, 15 February 2012 - YOU ARE STILL WHO YOU WERE 73
Friday, 17 February 2012 - NB. MISSING BLOGS 74
Friday, 17 February 2012 - MISSING LINKS 75
Monday, 20 February 2012 - VALLEYS AND HILLSIDES 76
Monday, 5 March 2012 - RAISING OTHER'S SPIRITS CAN
    HELP MAINTAIN YOUR OWN 77
Friday, 16 March 2012 - SPRING BRINGS NEW OPPORTUNITIES 78
Sunday, 18 March 2012 - RIDING THE WAVES 79
Monday, 2 April 2012 - SENIOR MOMENTS 80
Thursday, 26 April 2012 - RISKING EMBARRASSMENT 81

POEMS BY THE AUTHOR
CONTENTS

2011 85
    THE DAYS THEY ARE A CHANGING 85
    AUTUMN MUSES IN THE HILLS 87
    PREPARING FOR CHRISTMAS 88
    TALE OF TODAY'S AUTUMN SOJOURN (ADULTS
        AND YOUNG ADULTS ONLY) 90
    ADVENT 92
    STILL HE SLEPT 93
    SPIRITS OF CHRISTMAS 94

2012 97
    START OF A WINTER'S DAY 97
    ODE TO THE WETTON DROUGHT 99
    EARTH AND LIFE IN HARMONY 101
    LET THE LIGHT SHINE 102
    AUTUMN FALL 104
    ADVENT THOUGHTS 106
    ROOTS 108
    HOAR FROSTY MORN 110
    CHRISTMAS JOY 111
    YEAR OLD and NEW are NIGH 113

2013 115
    MID WINTER MUSE 115
    MISTS OF TIME 117
    SUCCESS and FAILURE 118
    HAPPY ST PATRICK'S DAY 119
    SPRING ARRIVES 120
    LIFE'S SEASONS 121
    SILENCE 123
    CHRISTMAS APPROACHES 124
    LIFE'S MYSTERY 125

I DON'T LIKE MONDAYS 126
THAT CELTIC HERO 127
THE EASTER FEAST 128
PRAY SILENCE! 129
WHO DOES NOT PRAY? 130
CHANGE 131
WAR 133
LITTLE WORLD 134
TAKING OURSELVES TOO SERIOUSLY? 135

2015 136
THOUGHTS 136
RISK TAKER'S PRAYER 137
OUR PEARL 138
SHORT THOUGHT 139
THE MOMENT 140
EASTER THOUGHTS 141
CYCLE OF LIFE 142
NOT TO DESPAIR 143
STRIVING 144
BIRTHDAY EVE 145
FATHER'S DAY MUSE 146
JUST A THOUGHT 147
STORMY WATERS 148
PAST, PRESENT, FUTURE 149
COURAGE IN CONFUSION 150
SPIRIT OF HOPE 151
ADVENT JOURNEY 152
BEING WHAT WE ARE 153
CHRISTMAS THOUGHTS 154
NEARLY THERE 155

2016 156
FED UP 156
HOME AT LAST 157
CYCLE OF LIFE 158
EASTER THOUGHTS 159
SPRING 160

ARISE AT DAWN 161
LET THEM BE 162
BANK HOLIDAY 163
CREATIVITY 164
CONVICTIONS.. 165
THERE IS A TIME 166
MOMENTS 167
EACH DAY 168
THE FUTURE 169
A MOMENT 170
LEST WE FORGET.. 171
CHRISTMAS CONTENTMENT.. 172
THE POLITICAL INCORRECTNESS 173

2017 174
    THOUGH DIVIDED, TOGETHER WE STAND 174
    ALLEGIANCE... 175
    THOUGHTS POLITICO 176
    HELP YOURSELF 177
    HEAR THE MUSIC 178
    POSITIVE THOUGHT 179
    WHAT TO MAKE OF IT ALL? 180
    VIEWPOINT... 181
    THE FUTURE 182
    AS UNDERSTANDING FADES 183
    HELP YOURSELF 184

ABOUT THE AUTHOR

Having initially worked in Banking and then Industry for six years, I spent the final thirty two years of my professional career, from 1974 until 2006, in senior managerial roles in the UK National Health Service.

Suffering two strokes in 2005, necessitated my early retirement in 2006. Having served fourteen years as Manager of Llandudno General Hospital and twelve as Chief Executive of St David's Hospice Llandudno, North Wales, life was then to change beyond recognition.

Within a matter of months following the strokes, I was diagnosed with early onset dementia. The diagnosis was received, a few days before my wife Sammy and I departed Wales to spend our planned retirement together, in the Peak District, Derbyshire, England, the county of our birth.

In view of the diagnosis and in retrospect, this move to the countryside, with our young Springer Spaniel, Blossom, was ideal, in so many ways.

We both loved rural life and after years of busy professional lives, my wife having been a secondary school teacher, it proved to be an ideal setting to make a start on life's new retirement journey, together.

An active and recuperative, number of years ensued, with daily walks over the fields with Blossom. My walking, aided by a shooting stick for periods of rest. These daily excursions, plus regular swimming sessions, gardening and looking after our hens, all provided for an idyllic retirement.

Although the daily activities possibly helped to delay the further progress of the disease, Sammy and I were becoming, increasingly, aware of it's slow, yet steady, advancement. This became a stark reality one Sunday morning, as a result of the following incident, that could have resulted in a tragic outcome, yet, fortunately, did not:-

For some reason, still unknown to me, I had put a saucepan of water on the lit gas cooker ring, just before my wife and I left to go to the village church for the morning service. Unfortunately I had forgotten to turn it off. A few minutes after the service started I returned to our cottage to get myself some tissues. On entering, and with Blossom lying asleep in her bed, I found the last few drops of water boiling away in the bottom of the saucepan....it was a narrow escape from what would have been a certain disaster.

This incident unnerved me considerably and was a sharp reminder of the implications of the dementing state.

2011 was a transitional year, as far as my, self help regime, was concerned. In July of that year, I decided to write a blog, entitled; "A Good Life With Dementia", not knowing over what period I would undertake the excercise. In addition, during September of that year I commenced writing some poetry.

The poetry, combined with the blog, that now form the contents of this book, were, originally, only shared with immediate members of my family. The blog, of course, already being in the public domain.

Five years later in 2016, I was referred by my doctor to a Consultant Psychogeriatrician for assessment. It was as result of this consultation, further memory tests and brain scans, that Alzheimers was formally diagnosed. (The disease from which my late father, Sydney Ashton, had died in 2002).

At this stage, a recently approved Alzheimers drug was prescribed, which I have, subsequently, continued to take, daily, at the maximum permitted dosage.

During the past four years, I have increased and extended the degree of activities undertaken. This includes, playing twice weekly sessions of walking football and attending a weekly choral singing group. In addition, since the recent sudden death of Blossom, our thirteen year old Springer Spaniel, I undertake five gym sessions per week.

The purpose of the above excercise regime, is to try and provide as much enjoyable, physical and mental conditioning as possible, with a view to staving off, the inevitable advancement of the Alzheimers disease, for as long as possible.

In the intervening period I have had a number of TIAs (mini strokes) but thankfully have recovered well following each incident.

Finally, I decided to arrange for publication of this book for the following reasons:-

1. To encourage other fellow members of the Dementia club to try and maximise their, undoubted, potential.
2. To provide a brief insight into the mind of one individual with the disease and his strategies for survival.
3. To take this opportunity to formally thank Sammy, my wife for her unstinting love and support and that of my family and friends.
4. To raise much needed funds in support of St David's Hospice and Helen's Trust Hospice, Derbyshire, England.

FOREWORD TO BOOK BY JOE SYDNEY ASHTON

Dementia is seen a scourge of our age. It creeps up insidiously and gradually erodes mental capacity, bringing with it stigmatisation and isolation.

Yet Joe has not shrunk away from this fate. He has faced it head on, while doing what he can to slow its progress. He exercises his body and his mind, and has developed coping strategies to ensure those around are not embarrassed by lapses in memory. We can find new richness in the world by seeing things though his eyes.

We all live with uncertainty every moment of our lives, yet we live as if we have control over things that happen to us. We certainly can control many of the trivia of life- what we chose to wear, whether we answer that phone call or not – but we cannot control whatever fate has in store for us: the accident, illness, infection, an error by someone else that results in injury or death. Perhaps an intrinsic failing of modern society is that we do not surrender to the forces that are far greater than our own willpower. We must recognise the intrinsic nature of uncertainty in every aspect of our lives, for only by doing that can we value the present to the full.

He writes with touching candour about his experiences. He questions without bitterness the word around him, aware of his limitations and the boundaries that are fractured by this condition.

Joe sees the beauty in the world around and the good in everyone he encounters.

Around him is rich world of experiences that are to be savoured, enjoyed to the full in the moment of today.

Joe has turned his experiences into a joyous recognition of the fragile and precious nature of life itself. Enjoy this book – for that is what Joe wants you to do.

Ilora Finlay
Prof Baroness Finlay of Llandaff FRCP FRCGP FMedSci FHEA FLSW
Professor of Palliative Medicine Cardiff University and
Chair of the National Mental Capacity Forum (England and Wales)

A COLLECTION OF BLOGS

By Joe Ashton

MONDAY, 4 JULY 2011

A GOOD LIFE WITH DEMENTIA

Six years ago, following two strokes, I was diagnosed with dementia and medically retired at the age of 58 years. A few months later, one of the physicians suggested that I consider setting up a blog. The reason he made this suggestion, was because I was increasingly finding it easier to communicate via email rather than speaking face to face with individuals and having a telephone conversation.

So, for whatever reason, I have today, six years later, been moved to take up the above suggestion. I am hoping that this exercise will be of benefit to both myself and maybe other dementia card holders and/or their carers. I experience and my ever caring, loving, wife has to share in my experience, of the majority of classic clinical symptoms of dementia.

I thank God, (I believe in God, but can assure you as many who know me will vouch, I am frequently not one of His or Her best representatives) that, so far, I am still enjoying a GOOD life, in spite of being aware and sometimes having to be made aware, of the ever creeping deterioration in a number of areas, e.g. acceptable/ unacceptable behaviour, (currently having issues regarding freedom of expression / rudeness to friends and acquaintances) and increased vocalised irritability. I am also currently trying to curb the unnecessary and inappropriate use of swear words, in place of thought out, appropriate responses. In spite of the above, life for me is GOOD, although this is tempered, on reflection, by the knowledge that life is not as GOOD, for those who have to cope with me. At the time, this behaviour seems to me to be reasonable and it is often only on reflection, or when pointed out, that I appreciate it wasn't.

In future blogs, I propose to share with any interested readers and with myself, personal insights / reflections on some aspects of both the positive and negative nature that the dementing state has had to offer so far. I hope that anyone who joins me on this blogged journey will enjoy the ride!

JSAFGA Posted by A GOOD LIFE WITH DEMENTIA at 13:19

TUESDAY, 5 JULY 2011

WHY AM I SHARING THE DEMENTIA JOURNEY?

Today I have to examine further, why I now wish to share with the world the dementia journey. I consider it important, for my own, as well as any potential readers sakes, to examine why I think this form of sharing is appropriate / necessary. Maybe it is a combination of ego, showmanship, wishing to tell my own story, rather than being the recipient of well-meaning health professionals' interpretation of where I am and where I should be. The filling of the void, between what was and what is. Maybe a wish to be more easily understood / to be more understanding. Possibly the hope that written expression will provide a deeper insight into where this journey is taking both myself and the passengers who are having to accompany me.

As mentioned in yesterday's submission, the suggestion regarding the possibility of my undertaking a Blog was made to me six years ago. It is only now that, for whatever reason, I have suddenly had the urge to write one. It is possible that, as I am becoming more aware of the developing nature of this state and it's effect on others, I have the need to open / broaden aspects of my communication, as other areas falter

The increased reliance on support, for this otherwise extremely independently minded individual, was further illustrated today, when having undertaken my first blog yesterday, I omitted to note the full blog address and therefore could not access it this morning. An SOS email to my granddaughter requesting HELP, eventually resulted in her somehow extracting the site details from the blogosphere. Hence my being able to post this submission today. Thank God for the caring, helpful, understanding folk, called grandchildren!!

JSAFGA Posted by A GOOD LIFE WITH DEMENTIA at 09:49

WEDNESDAY, 6 JULY 2011

DOES EXCERCISE HELP?

I am mindful that, as with many aspects of individual lives, there is no "one fits all" solution. This is particularly relevant regarding health issues. As we know, what works for one, is of no value to another. I therefore intentionally commence today's blog with acknowledgement that this is the case. I appreciate that, anything I state in these submissions that I find useful, will not be appropriate for others.

Following the two Strokes that preceded the official diagnosis of my dementia, I undertook numerous physiotherapy sessions in order to strengthen the left leg and to improve balance. This treatment was effective and in conjunction with it, I commenced a daily walking regime. This was enhanced by the purchase of a Springer Spaniel pup, Blossom, my constant / faithful walking companions these past 6years. Living in the hills, I take a shooting stick with me on each of the two daily walks we undertake over the meadows. This useful piece of equipment acts both, as a balance aide and also provides a seat, when required.

Irrespective of the weather conditions, snow, hail, rain, fog or shine, Blossom and I undertake a 1.5 to 2hour walk over the meadows each morning after a piece of toast and a cup of tea. This is followed by a further hour walk before the evening meal. The extremes of weather enhance the experience and a good supply of ex sailing, well insulated waterproofs and wellingtons, ensures that the weather is not permitted to spoil the enjoyment of our exercise. Having Blossom joining me on these exercise sessions is a real tonic and greatly enhances the experience. Watching her leap the stone walls, spring pheasant, chase rabbits and hare, provides a massive amount of joy and vicarious pleasure. This is further enhanced by the accompaniment of Pavarotti or Rolling Stones on the old MP3 player or listening to the radio while walking.

Joe Ashton

Sometimes, the music and radio are turned off, and time is spent sitting quietly, taking in glories of nature in silence and letting the mind blow in the wind. Out there in the hills, there are no concerns about having to focus on saying the right thing or upsetting others with an unwarranted outburst. There is only the wonder and beauty of creation at which to marvel. The stresses associated with occasional confusion, memory loss, the need to focus on essential undertakings and having to acknowledge you are not as you were, not as others once new you, are now gone - disappearing aboard the clouds as they float by. The blue sky, as it appears, provides a new hope/ optimism and realisation that each day STILL PROVIDES new opportunities to excel and to achieve. Not in the manner of one's former life, but, on good days, to explore new ways of maximising one's potential. Like Blogging for instance!! Enough for today!

JSAFGA. Posted by <u>A GOOD LIFE WITH DEMENTIA</u> at <u>13:48</u>

THURSDAY, 7 JULY 2011

THE BENEFITS OF EXCERCISE CONT

Today, I wish to continue the exercise theme and the benefits to me of the same. Initially, six years ago, the extent and duration of the daily exercise undertaken was extremely limited and was confined, at the time and for the first 12 months, to a gentle walk along the beach. This gradually built up, in the following 18 months, to going with Blossom for daily walks in the wooded area near home. In addition, a twice weekly swim in a local pool was added to the self-devised exercise programme. Walking was involved both too and from the pool. I could no longer drive, due mainly to concerns regarding the lack of spatial judgement and reflexes / reaction times.

Our move to the current home in the hills, facilitated a gradual increase in the amount of walking undertaken, to the present levels, combined with a weekly swim. In the past four years there have been two further TIAs. However, a rapid recovery, following each one, did not interrupt the daily routine for long. In addition, a limited amount of gardening is undertaken.

The significance of ensuring that I can undertake the above daily exercise routine is vital, as far as I am concerned. It has provided physiological benefits, including a stone weight loss and reduced breathlessness. Just as significant and equally beneficial, has been the psychological benefit the solitude and pressure free walks over the meadows with Blossom provide. Issues are able to be thought through, in a time free manner, facilitating a philosophical approach.

I have recently considered what the situation would be and how I would cope if, for whatever reason, I was no longer able to undertake the current level and type of exercise. It is a question that I do not find easy to contemplate. However, I do appreciate there are many dementia sufferers who can no longer undertake the activities that they previously could. In summary, my response to this question is to continue to adopt the current approach i.e. making the most of all the faculties and abilities I have available to me at the time.

Joe Ashton

The longer the gradual delay to the increase in the debilitating and incapacitating effects of the disease can be achieved the better. I am currently of the opinion, that in my case, exercise is greatly assisting the achievement of this objective.

JSAFGA Posted by <u>A GOOD LIFE WITH DEMENTIA</u> at <u>13:09</u>

FRIDAY, 8 JULY 2011

ISSUES REGARDING COMMUNICATION

There are, no doubt, a multitude of issues relating to communication, specifically associated with dementia.

The issues referred to above, will relate both to the dementing individual, the family, carer / carers, relatives, health professionals, friends, neighbours, members of the community in which the dementee resides, former colleagues, new acquaintances, members of the public, to name but a few!! In this blog, I will not be able to deal with all those mentioned, so will commence in the order stated.

From a personal perspective, the least stressful and the most fluent way for me to communicate is through the use of word processing and emailing, hence this blog. Even the daily one to one spoken communication with my wife, increasingly requires greater concentration on my part, to grasp what she has said and then to be able to make the appropriate verbal response or to undertake a task. A degree of checking out now has to be undertaken; to be sure I have correctly absorbed what has been said. It can occasionally, be even more confusing / stressful when a number of people are present and taking part in discussion. I use the word stressful advisedly, as there is a degree of stress and frustration brought on by not being as acutely aware and mentally alert in such circumstances, as one was in the past.

An associated example of the above, has occurred when my wife and I have gone out to town together and then arranged to meet up at a particular time and location. On a couple of occasions, due to my mild confusion, I failed to appear in the right place at the right time. As a result, I then started to write down the time and location where we were due to meet. However, we now always meet at the same location, quarter of an hour before the bus is due for the return journey. I have the bus timetable with me and therefore mark the time that the bus will be due to leave.

Joe Ashton

TIP:- Once a recurring issue has been identified, either by yourself or your carer, discuss it and together work out an agreed, simple, solution, as soon as possible. This helps reduce the frustrations, stresses and strains for all concerned, arising from recurring issues.

Wow, only dealt with some aspects of one issue re communication!! Enough is enough for today!

JSAFGA Posted by A GOOD LIFE WITH DEMENTIA at 12:23

SATURDAY, 9 JULY 2011

COMMUNICATION CONT

I have decided to be less specific than had been stated in yesterday's blog. It was going to be too complex and I do not feel up to attempting it for the time being. I will instead, give below, tasters of some of the categories of communicatees to which I referred: -

Majority of communication with the family, is done through email, as none of them live nearby, so that, fortunately, suits my preferred method.

Finding it difficult to continue with this communication section! On reflection, I suppose that this should not be too surprising, as it is one of the main areas of my life affected by the onset of dementia. I find conversation with persons who are not concise and get to the point quickly, quite irksome. I think this may be because of the difficulty I find trying to remain focused on what they are saying. This sometimes results in a brusque request / comment, to them to say what they mean. With people / friends who know me this now rarely causes offence, as they understand that I am trying to focus on what they are saying. Close friends have kindly adjusted their communication style accordingly, to compensate for my deficit in this area.

Being conscious that others have to adjust their method of communication for my benefit, while they are very kind for doing so, it is, nevertheless, annoying and frustrating, as it is a constant reminder of faculty diminution.

To date, I have found that shop assistants and the like have always been most understanding and helpful when, on occasions, I have had to deliberate on issues and been slower than others, to be able to communicate my requirements, or ask for clarification about what they have said.

It is probable that the increasing preference for periods of solitude rather than socialising, is the result of the issues surrounding communication. Reaction to people, situations and change, are diverse, to say the least!!

JSAFGA Posted by <u>A GOOD LIFE WITH DEMENTIA</u> at <u>15:03</u>

MONDAY, 11 JULY 2011

SECLUSION V ISOLATION

Today has been a reminder to try and get the balance right, if that is possible, between the benefits and peacefulness of seclusion in one's own quiet space and the risks associated with shutting oneself out from everyone and everything.

Fortunately, I am never totally alone, as Blossom, my springer spaniel companion, is constantly with me, whether we are out walking the meadows or when I am in my room relaxing, emailing, reading, watching TV or snoozing. The only place she does not accompany me, is when I am working in the garden, either cutting the lawn or on the veg patch. This degree of none verbal companionship has a lot to be said for it, in so far as, it does not present the type of stresses and strains that contact with other people, occasionally does.

I do not think it is particularly beneficial for anyone to be in total isolation other than for a very short period. However, a degree of occasional seclusion is likely to benefit most people. A time to switch off, to relax, to reflect on issues, to recharge one's batteries, to see a brighter horizon beyond the clouds.

I am currently having to work at getting, what for me will be, a healthy balance in relation to the above. Periods of seclusion can be interpreted as withdrawal and not wishing to communicate and to a degree, it is. However, not necessarily in the way that it might be perceived by others. I find it helps with, clarity of thought and presents the opportunity to sort the wheat from the chaff, in respect of so many aspects of human behaviour, including my own. However, too much seclusion could ultimately lead to isolation, which may then create far greater communication problems both within the home and with others. In summary, as with most things, a balanced approach usually results in the best outcome.

JSAFGA Posted by A GOOD LIFE WITH DEMENTIA at 12:36

TUESDAY, 12 JULY 2011

MAKING THE MOST OF THE NOW

The uncertainty of a long-term progressive condition, of indeterminable length and an unquantifiable speed of progression, presents one with the necessity to consider various options on how to deal with the situation. In my case, I was fortunate that dementia was diagnosed, as far as I can recall, only a few weeks before my wife and I were due to leave Wales, to move to our current home in the Peak District in England. We had, only a few months prior, decided to move away from the area, where we had spent nearly 30 years of our professional working lives. Now we were going back to our roots, nearer to the area we had left in 1977.

We had agreed that, under the circumstances, we would sooner make the enforced fresh start of early retirement in the countryside, in a village where we were not known to anyone. This move has proved to have been most beneficial for a number of reasons. These include the initial anonymity, which avoided the stress associated with necessarily coming into contact with former colleagues and other persons from our respective professional and social circle and endless explanations as to the why and wherefore that our lives had changed so dramatically plus the well-meant, yet unhelpful, commiserations.

We have been able, during this past four years, to settle in as members of a small village community, without the stresses and expectations of us, associated with life in Wales. We managed to do this initially by not informing anyone we were leaving and then only informing three or four close friends on the morning we departed. We new that from here on in we had to put ourselves first and that any upset that others might have, at not being informed we were moving or where we were going to, would have to be for them to deal with, as we had our own issues with which to cope!!

This was the start of the Making the Most of the Now. We now had to focus on dealing with this new phase in our life and having only recently received this latest item of medical luggage, we couldn't and were not prepared, to fit items of anyone else's in our Life's suitcase at that time. There are one or two individuals who still consider it was unreasonable that we did not say goodbye. However, I view that as their problem and hopefully, one day, they may resolve it, for themselves!!

When living on the coast in Wales, among the hobbies I particularly enjoyed were, sailing and fishing. Both these activities were governed by the changing tides. In analogous terms, I associate my dementia with the tide. High water was the day prior to diagnosis and fortunately, as far as my mental capacity at that time was concerned, it was a Spring tide, i.e. the highest of the year. It has, during the past few years, turned and is slowly retreating.

Often, when fishing from the shore, the largest fish are caught just as the tide turns and starts to go out. I am making the most of this exciting time, undertaking mental fishing, mainly through writing and meditation, and exercise, while out walking with Blossom over the meadows. I thank God that I have been given the opportunity to be able to undertake these pursuits that are enabling me to "MAKE THE MOST OF THE NOW".

I am, as with other dementiates, only able to be "MAKING THE MOST OF THE NOW", because I have a loving, supportive, caring, wife on whom to rely.

JSAFGA Posted by A GOOD LIFE WITH DEMENTIA at 14:04

THURSDAY, 21 JULY 2011

WE DO NOT HAVE TO RELY ON MEMORY TO ENJOY TODAY

Forget what you went into the pantry for? Oh yes frequently! Did you eventually remember what you were going there for? Oh yes after a while. How do you eventually remember what you were going there for? I retrace my steps to where I first started and then rather than struggling to remember, say a couple of unrepeatable expletives to myself, although all this does is release a bit of tension. Waiting there for a few quiet moments thinking of something else entirely, invariably frees up the mental block and I remember the reason for going to the pantry. The secret then is to set off post haste and get there before you forget again why you are there!!

Is the above frustrating? Yes, and upsetting, on the first few occasions. Can it be embarrassing? Yes, particularly if it is in connection with getting something for a visitor who does not know about your condition. Can you overcome the frustration and upset? Yes after a few occasions, if one conditions oneself to see it as a small rather than another big obstacle to undertaking daily routines. The challenge is to not let such events disturb one's equilibrium or knock one off course. Always remember, (no pun intended) that sooner or later you will invariably recall the forgotten thought.

Now, one can, rightly, argue that it is all well and good saying "chill you will eventually remember what it is you are looking after" etc. However, in many circumstances, these lapses of memory are extremely inconvenient and may have potentially serious implications / repercussions. Yes, this is true, like the time when, for no apparent reason, I put a pan of water on the stove and went off to church, having left it on the stove. Fortunately, on nearing the church, (maybe Divine intervention!) I realised I had left my spectacles at home, so I went back for them. On entering the kitchen, I saw the pan of water bubbling away with just a small amount of water left in it!! While turning it off, I could recall lighting it, but to this day, I still don't know why I put it on in the first place!!

Joe Ashton

Apart from the extreme type of memory lapse, referred to above, I now find that many of the lapses I experience, can be best managed in as calm and philosophical manner as possible. I am now at the stage, maybe dangerously so, of viewing such occasions as an opportunity to "move on", thinking of something else, not to dwell on the wrong note played by one instrument, but rather listening to the orchestra complete the piece. This "moving on" I find helps prevent getting bogged down by the stultifying frustrations of dwelling on what one has missed. Rather, I try and look for the next opportunity for the brain to focus on assisting with something positive / creative. This can be a reflection on happy memories of times past, the appreciation of the beauty of the present moment, or the anticipation that, for every major / minor slip up, there is still always another opportunity to broaden one's horizon.

WE DO NOT HAVE TO RELY ON MEMORY TO ENJOY TODAY!

JSAFGA. Posted by <u>A GOOD LIFE WITH DEMENTIA</u> at <u>14:38</u>

WEDNESDAY, 3 AUGUST 2011

LINKING THE PAST WITH TODAY

A couple of weeks ago, I joined a mass protest of 10,000 citizens in support of saving the Railway Company that is a major industrial employer in the area and is under threat of closure, with the loss of thousands of jobs.

The above event rekindled a multiplicity of memories of times in the 1970s, when I was employed for three years at the company concerned. At that time in the UK, a million people were unemployed, inflation was rampant, and many more jobs were under threat throughout the country. Rolls Royce the world-famous aero engine and motor car manufacturing, also based in the town, was about to go into receivership. It was only through mass protests and local cross-party political pressure and support, that the government of the day finally reversed its decision to let the company collapse and nationalised it. After not many years Rolls Royce was once more returned to private ownership and ultimately went on to become the world leading company it is today.

At the recent protest march, on seeing the banner of the trades union I belonged to 40 years ago, I was immediately drawn to walk in solidarity behind it, as in days of yore. I experienced a feeling of solidarity and comradeship, not only with those whose jobs are under threat today, but also in solidarity with the memory of former colleagues, many of whom are no longer alive, or too aged to attend, but who, had they been able, would have turned out to support the industrial family of Railway Employees in Derby.

The whole experience was a very moving and inspirational occasion rekindling the comradeship and togetherness that a cause of such significance to so many people's lives in the city engenders. It was as though the industrial relations battles of the 1970s, the government's mismanagement and resulting social injustices of the time, were once more having to be addressed, some 40 years later.

The above is a personal insight, NOT a political statement.

Joe Ashton

The day rekindled the flame of passion for a cause and the joy of solidarity. I have increasingly found that the linking of the past with the present, whenever possible, helps to make better sense of each. This I do best, when out walking over the hills with Blossom, my dog or when writing.

JSAFGA Posted by A GOOD LIFE WITH DEMENTIA at 12:54

TUESDAY, 9 AUGUST 2011

NO, ONE FITS ALL SOLOUTION, IN DEMENTIA

I do not prepare these blogs in advance and only give thought to what the content will be as the "New Post" sign comes up on the screen. This "go with the flow" approach, I find more inspirational and less mental blocking / stultifying than struggling with a planned /detailed offering. That form of approach now, I find can be quite frustrating, as the reduced concentration span in planned, formalised writing now, is stress inducing and stultifying and therefore not productive. Having spent my former professional life in necessary detailed planning as an essential feature, this alternative approach is proving to be the most satisfactory. However, although this approach suits me, it would obviously not be the case for others.

As the title of this blog indicates, each individual has to find their own best way of approaching issues. However, it is also the case that although one particular approach to situations may prove to be satisfactory one day, the same will not be the case on another day. One then has to try and adapt accordingly. In other words, flexibility has to be the name of the game.

Now, the above necessity for flexibility is all well and good for the dementiate. However, this does present difficulties for the carer. As there is no guaranteed, fixed pattern of behaviour or approach to issues, my wife has to be equally flexible in her response. A carer's lot is not always a happy one!

A frustration, I find, sometimes, is being aware that I am not always able to be consistent in many ways yet am unable to revert to type at that time. A high degree of self-awareness can be both a blessing and a curse at these times.

So, in summary, there is not a "one fits all solution" to many similar issues, even though the circumstances may seem to be the same. Unfortunately, one's response to situations cannot be reliably predicted.

JSAFGA Posted by A GOOD LIFE WITH DEMENTIA at 13:01

WEDNESDAY, 10 AUGUST 2011

TIME LOST TIME GAINED

I have just noted that these blogs commenced on the 4th July - Independence Day.

I am amazed that it is therefore only approximately six weeks since this journey commenced. If it had been indicated that my first offering had been made three or four months ago, that would have seemed reasonable - but six weeks, I find truly amazing. Is this of significance? Well yes to me it is, I am not sure why. A period of time that should be is not. A period of time that apparently has been, doesn't seem to be correct. This has just created a degree of uncertainty for me that I am currently NOW working through. There is a cloudy confusion at this moment that I am sharing and one that I know will lift at some stage, maybe in seconds, minutes, or hours, I do not know. How do I cope with this, what to do - keep calm enjoy the classical music that is playing, ironically entitled "Classical Chillout". I don't feel chilled out, there is an anxiety re confused time awareness. Sorry this has happened while blogging, but always have to go with the flow in trust that all will be well. The Beatles song "We Can Work It Out" springs to mind. As I carry on writing the significance of what it was that presented this issue is subsiding and although I recall it was about time lost and gained, I am managing to let it dissipate and a tranquillity / normality is returning.

The theme of Independence is one I will now focus on, possibly briefly, who knows!! The significance of independence is, I consider major. To be able to be as independent as possible, is an aim I focus on each day, being constantly reminded by my actions and reactions to people / situations, that like the memory etc, it has started, to ever so slowly ebb away. I will fight and am being lovingly supported by my wife, to retain as much independence as I can, for as long as I can. There are increasingly, more areas of life where I have to, unhappily, admit to not being able to cope with as independently as had always been the case in the past. I know what they are and don't intend to list them!! Why should I?

There are now different daily responsibilities that I hold on to and cherish, relatively minor as they may be compared to the responsibilities and drivers of my former professional life. However, in this life of NOW, they are, as I like to think and as my wife tells me, a significant contribution to our life. They are my daily drivers in to trying to maximise the use of the slowly dying wind that used to billow my sails and enable me to enjoy making the most of sailing close to the wind, both metaphorically and literally, in connection with work and when relaxing sailing.

Independence, self-respect and dignity are very closely interlinked. They are interdependent to a large extent and the diminution of one has an automatic knock on effect on the others. Start to lose independence and self-respect diminishes. If one's dignity is threatened, whether perceived or actual, then self-respect is also at risk. However, independence is retained at a price. One has to be constantly as focused as possible, so that one does not undertake or fails to remember to undertake, what is reasonably expected of one. This is a concern, when one knows from experience, that certain aspects of failed memory, or mildly unreasonable behaviour, demonstrated in either speech or acts, understandably, undermine the faith others can place in and the degree of independent latitude that should be afforded to you.

1. IS THIS A COMPLEX STATE?   YES!
2. ARE WE PROBLEM SOLVERS?   YES!
3. WILL WE MAXIMISE THE USE OF OUR RESOURCES TO DEAL WITH THESE ISSUES?   YES!

JSAFGA Posted by A GOOD LIFE WITH DEMENTIA at 13:11

SUNDAY, 21 AUGUST 2011

THREATS PERCEIVED OR OTHERWISE

Seems like have sailed into choppy waters this weekend, as when sailing in an area of wind against tide. Know the conditions will change, either the wind will shift direction and even if it doesn't, the tide will, eventually, turn.

Today, being a Sunday, maybe is a good day to consider the issue of Threats - Perceived or Otherwise.

What threats am I talking about? Well these come in many shapes and sizes and it is now becoming more difficult to differentiate between those that are perceived and those that are actual. There is a danger in getting them mixed up, as they are so significantly different in outcome, yet they can seem equally ominous, until unravelled. The difficulty is unravelling them!

What are the areas concerned?

   a. Credibility
   b. Integrity
   c. Reduced ability to understand / assimilate
   d. Others' perceptions of oneself
   e. Isolation

However, in the darkness of the moment, has come a ray of light from one of the village community, who, I consider to be a lighthouse / safe haven, the only one, apart from my wife, that is. A simple request for me to help him and his family in a small, yet meaningful manner. It is a major boost to one's confidence, self-esteem (not to be confused with ego), at such times, when one is acknowledged as being someone who can be of assistance. This is even more uplifting, when you know that they are aware of your having dementia. One cannot expect people to understand the complexities of the situation, when they are not experiencing it and when one does not fully understand it oneself. In spite of the few current issues referred to above, LIFE IS GOOD!

JSAFGA Posted by A GOOD LIFE WITH DEMENTIA at 12:20

FRIDAY, 26 AUGUST 2011

A TRUSTED, PROFESSIONAL EAR CAN ASSIST

Having experienced the development of a, less than tranquil transitional period, during the past few weeks, I considered it necessary to arrange an extended appointment, for a one to one discussion, with my GP the other day. It was the first appointment I have arranged with him, specifically, to discuss the dementing state, outside of my annual, general health, review.

It was a satisfactory consultation from my point of view. He did all the listening! It provided an important opportunity to update the GP on developments, from my perspective. Arrangements for professional counselling sessions, should I consider it appropriate at any time, are now being undertaken. This backup facility, I have been considering requesting for some time. Knowing that it will be available, should I wish to avail of it, is a great help.

There has been an increasing sense of an erosion of independence and reduction in one's ability to be in charge of one's destiny. Some of this has been real and some has, possibly, been more perception than reality. Being independent and even more importantly, in charge of one's destiny, is extremely important. I wish the same to apply, as far as is practically possible, at all the remaining developmental stages of my life. This is possible even within the confines of a residential care facility. Although not always the case, in these establishments, the emphasis should be on ascertaining and as far as possible, meeting, the needs of the cared for, as opposed to the needs / convenience of the organisation.

A sense of being misunderstood and misunderstanding others, is a complicated business, with which one has to deal. It is a challenging and complex business, under normal circumstances, yet even more complex now, at a time when keeping things uncomplicated and clear are essential to maximising function ability. In order to avoid the dangers of complexity, it is necessary to seek out individuals who have the ability and adaptability to "talk straight" and who I can know of you that you will "say what you mean and mean what you say". This is far more important now, than it was a couple of years ago. There is a risk, of which there have been a couple, of unfortunate incidents, where I have considered it necessary to tell individuals to do so. In social situations, this understandably, from their "normal" perspective, is considered "ungracious". Yes, that may be the case. However, I no longer, always receive or perceive things that people say and do, in the same way as I may have in the past. This applies to family, friends and strangers and therefore it is not that one group is singled out for special treatment, be it good or bad!

HOW TO DEAL WITH THIS IN A POSITIVE, PROBLEM SOLVING, MANNER?

A. Avoid, as far as practically possible, people (the number seems to increase) who you know seem to present such difficulties.
B. Find one or two individuals (they may be small in number) who you know do not present these problems.
C. Try and develop strategies for dealing with such situations, without causing offence.
D. Try and remind yourself that there was a time in the past when these individuals would not have seemed to present such difficulties for you. It is not that they who have changed - Accept, it is you that has changed! Nevertheless, don't beat yourself up about it. If the battery is losing its power, you can't expect the light to shine so brightly!

JSAFGA Posted by A GOOD LIFE WITH DEMENTIA at 08:24

MONDAY, 29 AUGUST 2011

VALUABLE v VIABLE

Comments increasingly heard, among non-medical, as well as medical persons, in relation to other human beings, both born and unborn, is whether or not these individuals are considered viable.

What one considers viable may depend on the value one attaches to the person concerned. Viability and value may be very closely linked, dependent upon the circumstances that necessitate or lead to the viewpoint being expressed, or the subject being considered. These considerations are undoubtedly going to tax the minds of our politicians and other decision makers in decades to come, particularly, as a result of the projected ageing population in the UK. We will all have to fight our own corner, as long as we are capable of doing so, either individually, or collectively, or probably a combination of both.

Will we be considered a drain on the community's resources, when we can no longer provide what is considered a valuable input into society? Will our viability be questioned by the decision makers of the day? Will the value of the input we made into society during our lives, when we were considered to be vital and valuable, as well as viable, be considered when our future is questioned/considered?

As we lie in the nursing home or hospital bed, hopefully, there will be someone around who will be in a position to point out to the young fit decision makers, that the person they see lying, silently, there is the same person others remember for his/her contribution to society, no matter how great or small it was. He /she is still a member of the human race. God considered him/her a valuable creation, whether born or unborn.

The above is possibly for the future. What about today? The object will be to ensure that, while one can, one maximises one's ability to provide a valuable role for one's family and leave concerns regarding the judgement of one's value, to God, who I believe is not interested in one's potential viability!

JSAFGA Posted by A GOOD LIFE WITH DEMENTIA at 07:44

TUESDAY, 30 AUGUST 2011

TODAY'S OPPORTUNITIES V THE REDUCTION IN YESTERDAY'S ABILITIES

One way to deal with reduced abilities is, rather than focusing on their loss, to find ways of creating new skills. This may or may not require new physical or mental agility or both. Where possible, try and counteract each loss, by creating a gain. One aspect of the slowly increasing dementing state, of which I am conscious and have also been made aware by others, is that of increased insensitivity in relation to others, which on occasions, understandably causes offence / upset. At the time of the incidents, the issue of others sensitivities is not considered a priority. A point has to be made or matter clarified, at that time. Sometimes, it is only on reflection and /or it being discussed calmly, at a later time, that recognition / acceptance of the inappropriateness of one's behaviour, occurs. What is the relevance of this in relation to the observation in the above paragraph? This is given below: -

The loosening up of one's sensitivity / verbal inhibitions, while disturbing to others, can sometimes be channelled positively. I have tried to do so recently through writing a couple of short children's stories. Though not great literary pieces, they have proved to be a method of using the simplest of subjects, i.e. wildlife, to develop / maintain the creative side of my personality that in the past was channelled into my professional working life. These stories have facilitated the ideal combination of the factual and the fanciful. This combination of aspects currently dominates my thought processes and to a greater or lesser degree must be influencing my behaviour towards and response to others. I lay great emphasis on individuals "keeping it real" talking straight and not wrapping things up in fanciful unreal language. The reason I require this to be so, is to enable me to, readily understand what is being said, as I now find it increasingly difficult to concentrate on trying to establish and listen to the "music behind the words".

The loss of the ability to focus and fully absorb what is being said is now being superseded by the attempt to counteract it through the development, however feebly, by this occasional writing of short stories for young children.

JSAFGA Posted by A GOOD LIFE WITH DEMENTIA at 14:09

… THURSDAY, 1 SEPTEMBER 2011

HUMOUR CAN BE A MASSIVE SUPPORT

Humour can be an incredible support for people in general and likewise with dementia.

Yes, you do run a risk that people will be laughing at you, rather than with you and that this can be a more of a behind the hand snigger rather than laughter of an appreciative nature at the real humour in situations. However, I believe this is a risk worth taking and whatever others views, may or may not be, don't let this apprehension stultify the growth and increased happiness / sustenance, that humour and laughter can bring, so what if some really don't find the comment or situation amusing? - that is their right. However, it is also your right to maximise the enjoyment of the humour, provided it is not at another's expense. I am moved to write this blog, following an incident that occurred earlier today, as detailed below:-

My wife was out visiting a neighbour when the phone rang. This is of significance as she will normally answer the phone if she is at home, mainly because I often have difficulty communicating fluently on the phone for any length of time and find it a strain.

On saying hello, the caller asked is it was Mr A, too which I replied "yes". He asked the same question again and at this point I thought I recognised the voice as that of a good friend from Wales. At this point, thinking it was my friend, I therefore replied in an oriental accent that it was the local village Chinese Laundry and that all white items of laundry should be kept separately from coloured items. I then asked the caller did he want to place an order and if he didn't to stop wasting my time and get off the line. At this point, there was a deafening silence, so I then asked in my normal voice if it was my friend Geoff. At this point the person on the other end of the line said; "Mr A, it is Dr H your GP here". When I confirmed to him that it was and that I had thought it was a friend ringing, he said "thank goodness for that, I thought you had gone really bonkers".

Ironically, my GP had rung to let me know that, following my request during a recent consultation with him that he enquire about the possibility of attending counselling sessions, if I considered that they might be helpful at some time, he was reporting progress. This had therefore been the purpose of the phone call from him to confirm that the local mental health team would be available if and when I wished to be referred for a counselling session. We were then both able to enjoy the joke re the identity mix up. However, I think he may now be relieved that he has made contact with the mental health team regarding myself!!

Interestingly, for my own protection, although I am anonymously prepared to share this event via this blog, I would not risk anyone, other than family, being made aware of the above event, as it would be likely, in my opinion, to further colour their perception of my mental state.

JSAFGA Posted by A GOOD LIFE WITH DEMENTIA at 12:40

FRIDAY, 9 SEPTEMBER 2011

PATIENT INVOLVEMENT IN EDUCATING HEALTH PROFESSIONALS

Today's blog has been prompted by a feature I read this week in a local newspaper, regarding the advances in Dementia care at a specialist unit. The above feature stated; "Staff even leave dusters lying around the wards so that patients can assert their independence and feel useful by polishing the furniture." If and when I have to go into one of these units, I hope that supportive developments in the field of specialist psychotherapeutic support for Dementia patients will have moved on considerably, from the stated practice of leaving dusters lying around for me to do a bit of dusting! I see this as a degrading and from my perspective can be described as lazy and unimaginative provision of care.

Apparently, the specialist caring innovations include: "Other ways to sooth patients include giving them pieces of cloth covered in buttons, zips and a variety of textured fabrics with which they can fiddle." I can think of nothing more agitating, than being presented with a load of buttons on a cloth, together with zips to attempt to undo. Having witnessed my late father, who had Alzheimer's, anxiously struggling with his key case and knowing that with its removal, he became less anxious, I am extremely concerned if the above kind of "specialist care" awaits me.

Interestingly / disturbingly, no reference was made to the difference in the provision of services for those in the relatively early stages of the disease's development and people who are suffering its advanced stage.

I am in two minds as to whether to contact the nurse in charge of the unit to offer her a relatively early stage dementia, patient's insight / observations. One reason I hesitate to offer my observations, is that, it is possible, should my observations be seen as threatening and unwelcome, my reaction could be unproductive. One of the by-products of the condition, that I have been increasingly aware of this past year, is that, increasingly, I can no longer confidently predict my response to people and situations.

As I write, I am now increasingly of the opinion, that it might be safer, for all concerned, if I were to forward my observations in writing to the unit.

Another frightening omission from the newspaper feature was the total lack of reference of the necessity to maintain a patient's dignity and self-respect. For people to be treated with dignity and to be able to maintain their self-respect, I believe, is essential in any health care setting.

Rather than dusting, patients should be offered the opportunity to commence blogging!

JSAFGA Posted by <u>A GOOD LIFE WITH DEMENTIA</u> at <u>13:06</u>

SATURDAY, 10 SEPTEMBER 2011

INTERTWINING THE PAST WITH THE PRESENT

Where we are today has been intertwined with our past influences, be it by people, places and a myriad of life experiences. It is therefore now great to be able to let them all come together in a gentle mix. This for me, is helping create many joyful periods and times, when alone in various places and settings, I draw on the past and blend it into today and this greatly enhances the experience and views of the past and present.

The above experience is not to deny the times of past unhappiness or trauma, but rather, not to feel the need to have them as a focus. Not to let them be a distraction from the beauty of each present day and the opportunities it presents to appreciate the overwhelming good memories of times past, both many years ago and also recent. The absent mindedness and occasional difficulties in verbal communications, maybe, lead to enhanced focus on the positive aspect of the many things I can do, rather than longing for the enhancement of past abilities.

Much appreciation and pleasure is gained from regularly visiting areas of the town where I was born and revisiting areas in the town centre. Although it has changed considerably from how it was in the 1950/60s, nevertheless there are some significant features that are unchanged and that have been splendidly blended in with the relatively modern buildings. It provides an excellent, gentle, eclectic mix of the past and the present, the yesteryear and the now. I find a regular couple of hours amble alone through the streets of the town centre, to be a most calming and rewarding experience. Seeing the people of today and at the same time enjoying thoughts of people I knew and well-known characters of the town from times gone by, is a most enjoyable experience.

So the D is seeming not only to be slowing aspects down, but more importantly, providing enhancement of other mental facets.

JSAFGA Posted by <u>A GOOD LIFE WITH DEMENTIA</u> at <u>14:13</u>

TUESDAY, 27 SEPTEMBER 2011

DONT FIGHT THE JOY OF PEACE

It occurred to me today, when out over the meadows with Bloss my Springer Spaniel, in the warm autumn sunshine, that the peace resulting from letting the mind go it's own way, in total peace and relaxation, should not be resisted. This regular feeling of peace is something I have increasingly experienced in the past couple of years, as dementia has progressed. Whether it because the increasing feeling of nothing much matters, or, possibly, that one's priorities have altered and become more relaxed and less complicated / complex. It is also probably assisted by the fact that my wife, of necessity, has had to take over the ultimate responsibility for affairs that, previously, would have been mine.

Keeping things simple and straightforward, while proving to be increasingly necessary to assist my understanding, is, I believe, having the knock on, yet beneficial, affect of removing the dross that might previously have made the contemplation of things, more complex than necessary. The mind currently thrives on the simple and straight forward, and yet at the same time, is opened up to many moments of quiet contemplation that result in, what appear to be, straight forward and simple insights into a variety of issues. This, in turn, provides a considerable degree of inner peace. I am of a mindset that why should one fight the joy of the peace that a simple and straightforward, yet insightful, approach to the contemplation of issues brings. In other words, keep it simple.

This season of autumn ties in quite nicely as to where I am in the normal life span and possibly in relation to my intellect. It has been an earlier intellectual autumn than I was anticipating, with the dwindling and reducing mental resources in relation to memory, understanding. However, these reduced faculties have, I believe, been compensated by the development of new creative, insightful, peaceful, contemplative, abilities, that, as far as I am aware, have developed.

Joe Ashton

To those fellow sharers in the world of dementia, might I respectfully suggest you try not to fight the joy of the peace you may, at times, experience? Yes, you can't do what you did. Yes, you can't be the way you were before. Yes, you have your moments of frustration and annoyance at your state. Yes, you have feelings of sorrow and helplessness. Yes, you are annoyed and frustrated that you have to be reliant on your loving carer. Yes, you may fear the potential results of the strain on your carer, that carrying out their support of you may bring. However, examine the potential benefits for yourself and your carer that periods of mind clearing peace will have. Then seek opportunities to facilitate it - Good Luck and Happy Hunting - IT WILL BE Worth IT!

JSAFGA Posted by A GOOD LIFE WITH DEMENTIA at 10:27

FRIDAY, 7 OCTOBER 2011

APOLOGISING FOR PAIN CAUSED

Recent experienced the pain of the realisation of the depth of pain and insult that one has, potentially, caused when unreasonably giving a short, yet unnecessary verbally abusive outburst. I delivered an unsolicited, humble, apology at the first opportunity the following day. It was only then on reflection that it dawned on me that what I had said was totally unreasonable. The problem is that at the time of these occurrences, one reacts instantaneously and without considered thought. This unfortunately is an increasing happening and at the time seems a reasonable knee jerk reaction. It is only on reflection that one is mortified by what one has said. Fortunately, the victim of the unreasonable tirade accepted the apology instantaneously and gave the gracious / consoling response of "that's fine, forget about it". Of course, one knows, on reflection, that what one had said was most unreasonable.

The above has been an increasing phenomenon, particularly with my ever-loving carer, my wife. Fortunately, we are so close and she is so understanding, that I am almost instantly aware of the inappropriateness of what I have said and readily apologise very quickly.

Apologies, although releasing, also have a pain full aspect, namely the realisation of the inappropriateness, unreasonableness and hurt caused by what has been said. The reflection on the situation is a constant reminder of the creeping and ever developing affects that Dementia brings.

The result of the above incidents is to make one less inclined to wish to socialise and become more isolationist, for fear of the hurt and chaos that inappropriate responses / outbursts cause. This is a tricky phase of this disorder. I say disorder rather than disease, as the state that it brings is one of increasing disorder for the owner of the condition and possibly even more so for the carer and friends.

This blog is entitled "A Good Life with Dementia" and yes in spite of the condition / disorder, life in general is good. However, I cannot forget that

Joe Ashton

while 90% of the time this is the case, the occasions of unreasonableness do not provide a good life for my wife, family, friends and even casual acquaintances. Those who are aware of the proximity of the condition are on their guard and to them certain behaviour / verbals do not come as a surprise and they appear to cope with them.

People are very kind and understanding. My wife and carer is an Angel.

JSAFGA Posted by A GOOD LIFE WITH DEMENTIA at 05:30

TUESDAY, 18 OCTOBER 2011

"I WAS GOING TO MAKE YOU REMEMBER IT!"

A well-meaning, yet, as far as I am concerned, misguided, in fact, though not her fault, totally unguided, yet well intentioned, new neighbour, who is a relatively now friend of my wife's, knocked at our door two days ago. Our dog Blossom did her usual protective routine of barking a warning. This she usually does until I say; "it is alright it is only, (then I name the person) and let them in. Blossom then knows all is well and settles down. On this occasion, I couldn't remember the neighbour's name and called to her to remind me of her name. However, she did not respond and so I had to open the door and let her in anyway. When she had come, in I recalled her name. I told her that I was asking her to remind me of her name because I had forgotten it. To which she replied; "I know you had, and I was going to make you remember it". I let her know in no uncertain terms (only a few minor expletives) that doing that was of no help whatsoever and never to do it again. I further pointed out that if I asked for assistance to recall her name, I needed it, as didn't do it for the fun of it.

I have a feeling that having got to know this well intentioned, though as far as I am concerned unhelpful, individual, sufficiently well, that she will still consider she was being helpful and is likely to carry on regardless. If this is the case, then in a similar situation, the door will remain unopened with her on the other side!!

Now, as mentioned above, I am sure the lady's intentions were honourable and that she genuinely thought she was being of help. In the situation I find myself in, with this condition, I am not prepared to be used by some well-meaning, yet, to me, dangerous individual, as the object of their experimentation to try and cure my memory problems. I have detected from previous conversations and in getting to know, as well as observe, the individual concerned, that she is of the "I can fix anything" category of person. In order to avoid potential

Joe Ashton

conflict when she visits our home, having exchanged pleasantries, I now take my leave and seek the refuge of my apartment / relaxation room.

As certain aspects of my mental condition slowly change, I am aware that I seem to be becoming more frequently involved in conflictual and stress inducing and creating situations with others. These are usually as a result of my response, (seemingly to me reasonable at the time) to what others say or do.

Wishing to avoid the above and to minimise unsavoury incidents and resulting cause of hurt to others and myself, I spend an increasing amount of time out walking with Blossom our dog and limiting the amount of time spent in others company indoors. Interestingly, on reflection, I find it better to converse with individuals in the open air in the village, rather than in an enclosed environment, e.g. home, church, pub, etc. Thank God, from my perspective, I am at my most peaceful and relaxed when in the haven of our home, alone with my wife and Blossom, or when out walking alone or with Blossom.

JSAFGA Posted by A GOOD LIFE WITH DEMENTIA at 10:50

THURSDAY, 20 OCTOBER 2011

TRUST IN OTHERS UNDERSTANDING

As one becomes gradually less patient and amiable in many situations, one has to increasingly rely on the good nature / understanding of those who know you and others you meet. It is not a right to expect them to be good natured or understanding in relation to what may be perceived by the recipient as an unreasonable or less than diplomatic remark or comment.

When remarks or comments are made, as referred to above, at the time the comment is made, I consider it reasonable in the circumstances. Unfortunately, this is apparently not always the case and it is in those circumstances, that one has had to trust in the understanding nature of the recipient. My poor wife has had to develop an inordinate increase in diplomatic skills in order to quickly heal any wounds inflicted on the unfortunate recipients.

The strange dichotomy dementia has provided me, has been the opening up of a greatly broadened view on many issues, some of which I would have previously had a much narrower / dogmatic view. On the other hand, I increasingly rely on quite detailed specific information / instructions on a number of daily issues, without which confusion reigns. The development of a freedom of the mind to explore all sorts of thoughts and methods of expression on the one hand, yet a reliance on virtual hand holding in respect of a number of matters / issues, previously undertaken for years without any requirement for support. It is not easily understood!

The above leads to the option of more seclusion and the safety of the limited number of persons I consider I can rely on to trust in their understanding.

JSAFGA Posted by A GOOD LIFE WITH DEMENTIA at 12:57

FRIDAY, 21 OCTOBER 2011

CARING FOR YOUR CARER

While having my evening meal, I was mind full of the opportunities that are presented daily to provide my carer, in my case, my wife, reciprocal elements of care for her. Maybe it is the fact that I have always been less than useful in the cooking department that inspired such thoughts. This issue, (not the inability to cook) may also resonate with some fellow members of the "dementia club" and their carers. No doubt, the majority of us greatly appreciate how our carer and others, support us on this weird and sometimes, wonderful or less wonderful journey. Even those in a more advanced stage of the illness, who unfortunately are no longer able to communicate with their carer, may well still be aware that they are being cared for, even though they may not necessarily always be able to indicate that they know who it is that is looking after them.

I do not know, but maybe in cases where one's carer is a loved one, possibly it is more likely that one will be more inclined to seek opportunities to lighten their burden, than would otherwise be the case with a professional carer, be it at home or in a residential setting. Sometimes, I will do so without thinking. For example, undertaking simple tasks that my wife would otherwise have to undertake. This is of course easier to do some days than others, dependent on my state of mind and confidence to feel able to carry out the task successfully. In my case failure to deliver the goods, results in a considerable disappointment and resulting loss of confidence. Unfortunately, this impacts on the willingness to attempt the same task again, at a future date. There will sometimes be a willingness to try again, but then, when venturing further to carry it out, a sense of anxiety can pervade, resulting in an inability to undertake the task concerned.

An instance of the above that I experience, is the use of the telephone. For example, to ring up to make an appointment, is an area where I now rarely get involved. The reason being, if the person concerned on the other end of the line needs more than a couple of items of information from me, then unfortunately, this, increasingly, has me floundering and I will have to call my wife to bail me out. Therefore, all the well-intentioned thoughts of assisting her, by making the call in the first place, have not produced the desired result and have in fact only added to her burden. So now, unless I am feeling supremely confident on the day concerned, I avoid making telephone calls. Having reached this point, I think it more productive for both myself and my wife, that I don't beat myself up about the issue, but move on to find other areas where I can be of real assistance. Fortunately, I am relatively well, physically, thanks to the aid of medication. I therefore seek out physical jobs to undertake that need doing and that will be of help. Some of these are simple daily routine items and others are less frequent, yet equally important.

In trying to achieve a good life with dementia, those of us who are able, can continually search for ways of assisting this process for both ourselves and our carers. However, should we attempt new ways, or re-try old ones and fail, try not to become too despondent, find something new to ACHIEVE.

JSAFGA Posted by A GOOD LIFE WITH DEMENTIA at 11:57

TUESDAY, 25 OCTOBER 2011

KEEPING A POSITIVE OUTLOOK

There are many differing strategies people adopt in order to try and stay positive to help survive all sorts of situations life throws at them. Many people cope with situations on their own, or through the help of family, friends or health professionals. However, although they manage to cope, this does not necessarily mean to say that they consider they have a "Good Life". There are many people who, unfortunately for them, are not able to enjoy the benefits of a positive outlook when dealing with adversity. If anyone reads my blog who is in this category, I should point out that, although I am one of the lucky ones who has an innate positive attitude to life, I appreciate that many individuals who although they would possibly like to be able to adopt a positive attitude to adversity, find it extremely difficult, if not impossible.

An approach I find helpful in maintaining a positive attitude, is to avoid focusing on aspects of life that I am no longer able to undertake, or to take part in. Instead, I now focus on what I can do and look for opportunities to try and increase their variety and range. This does not always have to be something physical. It is often an inspirational thought process resulting from a quiet moment listening to a piece of classical music. The writing of a letter to a politician or sometimes royalty or other a world leader, expressing my thoughts on issues. To some this may seem a strange thing to do. However, my attitude is, if I find it helpful, I DO IT!

Another aspect to retaining a positive attitude and enjoying a good life, in spite of the dementing process, is to be able to maintain a sense of humour. When possible have a laugh at yourself, particularly about issues that were not amusing at the time and which possibly involved a stressful situation for both yourself and for others, as a result of your action. The following incident last week caused a considerable degree of stress for myself and both stress and embarrassment for my wife and a visitor to our home. However, now, a few days later, a description of the incident to visitors by both my wife and myself, enabled us to see the funny side of the incident and on my part, acceptance that, although there was a logical reason for my reaction at the time, on reflection, I acknowledge that had a similar occurrence happened a few years ago, I would have dealt with the situation in a far more diplomatic manner.

To be able to look back on incidents, as above, and to be able to see the funny side (if not viewed as funny at the time) is another major contributory factor to helping keep a positive attitude.

JSAFGA Posted by <u>A GOOD LIFE WITH DEMENTIA</u> at <u>14:05</u>

SATURDAY, 29 OCTOBER 2011

A GOOD WEEK

This past week has once more been a good one. What constitutes a good week for me? As far as I am concerned it is when the positive aspects outnumber the less positive. This criterion is possibly applied by most people when assessing the type of week they have had. The possible variable is what each individual considers to be "good".

A good week for me is one where I have managed, as far as I aware, not unreasonably, caused any offence to anyone with what I have said. I say unreasonably, as there are times when I consider that something has to be said, or a point made, which can upset the recipient, even though this is not the intention. I find that, increasingly, this is becoming an unfortunate aspect of my life. What is the alternative? Not be true to how you feel or perceive things? I do not think so! That would be totally alien to me both the person I am now and also the person I have been all my adult life. I find it increasingly difficult to be diplomatic, as opposed to being direct and truthful about how I feel. Anything less than an open and direct approach, presents the risk of confusion and increased frustration.

There were a couple of incidents this week, when, as far as I am concerned, what I said was reasonable in the circumstances. One of the recipients no doubt will not think so and the other will probably not care or be too concerned. On balance, a good week has been enjoyed.

JSAFGA Posted by A GOOD LIFE WITH DEMENTIA at 08:38

SUNDAY, 30 OCTOBER 2011

ADAPTABILITY HELPS

Events that occurred today have prompted this blog. In recent days we have had a new batch of young cows come into the field at the back of the converted barn in which we (my wife and I) live. They are particularly inquisitive and have taken to not only peering in through the windows that overlook the field, but also to noisily licking the window frames and the glass. This has been particularly annoying for our Springer spaniel, who dislikes the look of the huge bovine head peering in at her. Events went a stage further today when as a result of the satellite television signal being lost we have been unable to watch any TV. On inspection of the wiring outside, I found a large section of cabling had been chewed by our friends (the cows)! We will now be without TV for a couple of days before the TV Company can send someone to make a repair.

In view of the above, we have had to adapt to the new circumstances the cows have inflicted on us. My wife is still able to watch DVDs and I am enjoying listening to music Cd's. So, a whole new way of entertainment has had to be found to temporarily replace the former.

The changed circumstances and the need for adaptability in the situation have strong links to the provision of a "Good Life With Dementia". The necessity for one and one's carer to be able to adapt readily to changing circumstances is of great benefit. However, strangely, I now find it increasingly more difficult to adapt to changing circumstances and arrangements. Certainty is now the main provider of solace and peace. The necessary adaptability that uncertainty or changed plans required was something on which I used to thrive, both in my professional and personal life. Not so, today though, I am afraid. However, this temporary enforced loss of TV entertainment will be an interesting test in adaptability!

JSAFGA Posted by A GOOD LIFE WITH DEMENTIA at 15:24

WEDNESDAY, 2 NOVEMBER 2011

PEOPLE WITH DEMENTIA ARE NORMAL

People who have dementia are not special. We are normal individuals whose brain is degenerating at a greater pace and in some cases earlier, than most other people. I make the point about normality, as I think too greater emphasis is often placed on the differences between people with the disease and those without it. It is far easier and for some, a great defence mechanism, to emphasise the differences, rather than acknowledge similarities with someone or something one doesn't fully understand or feel comfortable with.

It would be helpful, for all concerned, if greater emphasis was placed on the similarities between patients, carers and health professionals, rather than the differences. This is not to deny that the dementia sufferer presents for others a number of specific issues / difficulties. Similarly, dementing individuals also have to cope, in a different way, with aspects that these issues present for them. In many respects therefore, this is the same for everyone else. In society, everyone has to adapt and make allowance for others in their personal and professional lives. To progress, in situations, the most successful outcome is achieved when differences, although acknowledged, are not the focus, the emphasis being on the areas of shared interest and mutual benefit.

Notwithstanding the above, my observations, are, possibly, prompted by the slight frustration of having to accept the difficulty, that one's response to certain situations, is not what one would "normally" have had a few years ago. In spite of this, the good aspects of each day usually far outweigh the less desirable.

JSAFGA Posted by A GOOD LIFE WITH DEMENTIA at 14:04

FRIDAY, 4 NOVEMBER 2011

A SMALL TRIUMPH MEANS A LOT

The title of today's blog is born of an incident that occurred yesterday, when using some former skills, I was able to resolve a problem.

We had been having a problem with our sky TV and the intermittent loss of our broadband Internet connection. This has been the case for a week and in spite of several calls by my wife and carrying out verbal instructions via the telephone, the problem was not being resolved. The fifth call yesterday morning to yet another different respondent, resulted in my having to speak to the person concerned. The full details of the telephone call I am unable to recall. However, I am able to say that I managed to stay calm and adopted a communication technique, used on many occasions during my former professional life, which resulted in the individual concerned taking the necessary action that resulted in an engineer visiting our premises this morning and quickly repairing the faulty connections. The small triumph referred to above therefore, was not only the satisfactory outcome in relation to getting the connection problems resolved, but on a personal level to have the satisfaction of having been able to satisfactorily use a former communication technique to good effect. A relatively small triumph of this nature may not seem much to the reader. However, it has given me a psychological boost as it is refreshing to be able to enjoy what I consider a minor triumph, as opposed to the numerous minor, yet mainly untoward, incidents in which I have been involved.

It is always good to be able to have some positive aspects to focus on as opposed to negative.

JSAFGA Posted by A GOOD LIFE WITH DEMENTIA at 05:04

SATURDAY, 5 NOVEMBER 2011

ENJOY THE COMPANY OF THOSE WHOSE COMPANY YOU ENJOY

Yesterday we had a pre-arranged visit from a longstanding friend, who together with Lynne, his now deceased wife, had been friends of my wife and myself since our teenage years. Lynne had been a bridesmaid at our wedding 42 years ago. We arrange to meet up about three times a year. These meetings were always in the past joyous and fun filled days and now continue to be with Clive, even though Lynne is no longer with us.

I mention the above, as these visits have always been for me, what I can only describe as "safe". Now what do I mean by "safe"? Safe in so far as there is no feeling of anxiety prior or during our time together. I consider them to be times of complete acceptance of each individual present, treating each other as we always have done, with openness, honesty and loving care. This is not to say that when other people visit some of those elements will not also be present, to a greater or lesser degree. However, we have always been able to accept each other as we are at the time on the day in question - no judgements, no directions, just acceptance of how we are and where we are at on that particular day. This make the company of these people joyous, non-judgemental and non-stress inducing.

I find it is now best to have, what I consider, a small number of quality friends, rather than a large number of friends. This may be a bit of an isolationist approach; however, it is one with which I consider most fulfilling. This does not of course rule out the acquaintanceship of other people either in the community where one lives or elsewhere. However, the problem I find with interaction with this category of person, is that there is a far greater risk of upsetting them and misunderstandings arising - not necessarily their fault, sometimes mine, nevertheless, problematical all the same.

So, today, I am definitely of the opinion that, for me, and possibly for others, the safest and most productive way forward, is to enjoy the company of those, whose company I enjoy.

JSAFGA Posted by A GOOD LIFE WITH DEMENTIA at 07:12

SUNDAY, 6 NOVEMBER 2011

TRYING TO AVOID THOSE WHO BRING THE WORST OUT IN YOU

One of the benefits of leading a more reclusive lifestyle, is minimising the opportunity for confrontational situations. There are of course issues that adopting this strategy presents. You may be viewed as isolationist by some in the community. You may also be viewed as a bit odd by some. However, maybe this is the lesser of two evils, namely, better that they view you this way, rather than they insist on making contact that is likely to result in confrontation and upset.

At this stage of the dementing process, while still living at home, the above avoidance is relatively easy for me to organise. In general, I have the freedom and ability to decide whether or not I come into with individuals. However, for the dementing person in residential care or even attending day-care, it is not so easy for those persons to avoid contact with certain members of professional staff responsible for their care, who may have a similar effect on them. This is something that, unpalatable as it may be, caring professional staff, both medical and nursing, should consider.

It will not be easy for most doctors or nurses to be able accept that, in spite of their professional qualifications and experience, because of how they present themselves as individuals to the patient concerned, they will, in some instances, be more of a hindrance to the patient's wellbeing, than help. I recall when my late father, an Alzheimer patient, was in the nursing home, shortly after admission, he used to react particularly badly in the presence of one senior nurse, namely the nursing home's Matron. She was just as caring as any other members of the nursing staff. However, possibly it was her accent and her voice, as opposed to what she said, that for whatever reason, he used to find disturbing. Fortunately, she quickly realised that this was the case. However, rather than letting any professional dignity or personal pride stand in the way, she minimised her personal contact with my father, while at the same time keeping a very close watch on the provision of his care by the nursing staff responsible for his care. This was of course the correct action for her to take.

Increasingly, I experience situations where, for no apparent reason, I find it difficult to be able to put up with people, without reacting, sometimes inappropriately. However, I am able to try and avoid such situations, or people with whom I react badly. People who are receiving residential care, are not able to do so. An understanding and empathetic approach by the health professionals providing their care, is therefore essential. They should be made aware as part of their basic and ongoing professional education, that specifically with dementia patients, the scenario that something as simple as their accent may possibly be the catalyst to unwittingly cause distress to their patient. When this is suspected, appropriate staff changes should be made.

A patient's wellbeing must always take priority over a health professional's pride!

JSAFGA Posted by A GOOD LIFE WITH DEMENTIA at 12:29

MONDAY, 7 NOVEMBER 2011

CARER TRUST

Today, I went to hospital with my wife (my Carer), as she was having a pre-operative appointment, in anticipation of her undergoing an investigative procedure, under general anaesthetic, on Thursday. I was delighted that she agreed to me accompanying her into the consultation. Understandably, at my suggestion, it was on the understanding that I say nothing when she was with the specialist nurse. My wife did however say to me that if there was something, I thought important that she might have omitted to say, then I should do so. This was a tremendous demonstration of trust and faith on her part, that she was prepared to risk my being present. (I use the word "risk" advisably, as I acknowledge, there was an element of risk involved on her part) However, I am delighted to report that the consultation proceeded without a hitch and I was even able to assist, when asked by my wife to confirm some information that was required.

Now, one may ask why did the above mean so much to you? Well, t demonstrated to me that in a potentially risky situation, my wife was still able to place her trust in me that I would be able to behave as agreed. The fact that I did so was a relief to her and to me! Unfortunately, these days, I cannot accurately predict what my response will be in different sets of circumstances and so this was a very special and morale boosting occasion. On Thursday, when my wife goes to the hospital for the, day case, procedure to be carried out, a friend of hers will be taking her and bringing her home. I will be at home walking the hills with Blossom, our Springer Spaniel, eagerly awaiting her return.

Coincidentally, on the early morning TV news programme today, there was a gentleman with Alzheimer's, who was in the studio with his carer wife. They were being interviewed live regarding how he had been diagnosed and how they managed the disease. It was good to see this gentleman describing, quite clearly, some aspects of issues involved re the circumstances surrounding events which eventually resulted in his diagnosis and the involvement / lack of involvement of health professionals. Anyway, seeing him gave me added encouragement and incentive to accompany my wife to the clinic today.

So I hope, that in the same way, these blogs may be not just a beneficial expressive release for myself, but possibly, also, a use full / helpful insight and encouragement for others on the dementia journey, their carers and maybe even health professionals with an interest in the subject.

JSAFGA Posted by A GOOD LIFE WITH DEMENTIA at 11:52

WEDNESDAY, 9 NOVEMBER 2011

HELPING YOUR CARER NOT TO WORRY

I choose this blog title today, as it is topical to me and my wife's (my carer) current situation. She goes into hospital tomorrow morning for an exploratory procedure that is usually undertaken on a day case basis, although the hospital have warned her that, as she is undergoing a general anaesthetic, she may have to remain in overnight. However, in view of her being my carer, she has been put first on the list, so they are hopeful she will be sufficiently recovered to come home later in the day. A good friend, who we jokingly refer to as "the carer's carer", is taking her and bringing her home. She is also meant to be keeping a watchful eye over my wellbeing, while my wife is away.

This situation has highlighted a few issues posed from my perspective, regarding the acceptance / acknowledgement of the need to have someone officially nominated as my carer and the fact that it is considered that when they are temporarily unavailable, that someone else has to deputise. I know that logically this should be the case. However, logic does not always concur with raw emotion. To have to acknowledge that this type of watching cover is necessary is not that easy to deal with in reality. The only reason I am trying my hardest to outwardly accept the arrangements made, is purely for my wife's sake, so that she will not be worried about me while she is in hospital, even if only for 24hours.

Of course I know and will acknowledge, when being completely honest, the risk elements that exist and make the necessity for this type of caring cover to be provided - Leaving pans on the cooker unattended and forgotten about, forgetting to take medication, dealing, sometimes inappropriately, with other people and upsetting them, difficulties sometimes experienced in dealing with phone calls. These are, unfortunately, some of the issues that make the arrangements above, necessary. The most important one of all, trying to relieve the burden of additional worry that my wife would otherwise incur.

One of the most baffling aspects of dementia to me is that I can happily write a blog of this nature and many other pieces of writing, without any problem, while at the same time experiencing the above issues!

Dealing with these issues / frustrations as calmly as possible is an essential requirement, to ensure that both patient and carer experience "A Good Life With Dementia"!

JSAFGA Posted by A GOOD LIFE WITH DEMENTIA at 07:51

FRIDAY, 11 NOVEMBER 2011

UNFORSEEN BENEFITS OF SHUTTING DOWN

This foggy, late autumn day has inspired today's blog. The meadows and surrounding hills have been shrouded in a thick blanket of fog all day. The walk with Blossom this morning had a different dimension to it, with cows and sheep appearing and disappearing in and out of the mists as we passed.

Knowing what would normally be visible in the different areas, yet could not be seen today, it struck me that in a similar way, the memory and thought processes and even conversations, nowadays, sometimes take on aspects of vision, both internal and expressed externally, which may cloud what is really meant to be said and what is sometimes lost, if only temporarily. In a positive vein, the vagueness and sometimes foggy thought process can possibly be beneficial, if accepted as a benefit. This can happen, if one can overcome the often-immediate associated response of frustration, sufficiently, to stop and let the brain take the time out it is apparently asking for, rather than making it continue to frustratingly struggle. Once cerebral equilibrium has been established, new and totally unassociated thought processes can emerge that take one on a completely different cerebral journey. The clouds of the mind slowly lift and reveal beautiful new horizons, some of which you had not previously seen, or viewed in this new way.

The above experience is similar to the way that the fog and mists of today, shut out the normally beautiful views. Yet at the same time, it helped inspire thoughts about the opportunities and potential benefits of giving the brain, temporary shutdown / recovery time, which can then facilitate the development of further new inspirations.

I should point out that the words "inspire" and "inspiration" are used advisedly. I am mindful that the personal illuminations described, and their resulting expression will possibly only serve to create a thick fog / mist and even blurred understanding / misunderstanding for those not sharing the dementing process.

JSAFGA Posted by A GOOD LIFE WITH DEMENTIA at 07:53

MONDAY, 14 NOVEMBER 2011

A SILENT FRIEND

The advantages and benefits of close friendships are numerous. However, I also greatly appreciate the benefit of having a loyal, trusted, yet, silent friend. One who listens, who is always there. One who usually responds to requests / directions, without explanation. One who always defends in times of potential danger, whether real or perceived? One who trusts you to have done and to do, whatever is required. One who does not need to check to see whether or not you have taken your tablets or whether you have left something on the cooker. One who does not have to worry whether something you say, in company, may offend. One who is not concerned if you stay out for an extra hour or so, when walking in the meadows. One who does not proffer unsolicited, although possibly well meaning, advice. The silent friend to whom I refer, of course, is Blossom, our Springer Spaniel.

Now, I appreciate that it is easy for a dog to provide uncomplicated companionship. As an animal, she has few needs to be met and is easily pleased. Yet she is a significant member our family unit. The many hours I spend each day out walking the hills, are enhanced significantly by the attendant company of Blossom. To watch her running in the meadows, as I walk, leaping walls, chasing rabbits and other wildlife, springing pheasant etc, provides an extraordinary amount of pleasure and mental stimuli. Whatever the weather conditions, the fun and joy of these daily walks are greatly appreciated and are to be savoured. It is hoped that at some far distant date, when they cannot be undertaken, the memories of the joy our "Silent Friend" brought, will never be forgotten.

JSAFGA Posted by A GOOD LIFE WITH DEMENTIA at 06:01

WEDNESDAY, 16 NOVEMBER 2011

RESPECT

Today's fog and mists have not clouded the thought processes, I am pleased to say. Out walking, I pondered the different responses I get from various individuals in the community in which I live, when I communicate with them and they with me. I am aware that what I say, or my reactions to what others say to me, will automatically influence their response and their view of me, as is the normal human response in the communication process.

The most significant issue of all, in the often complicated situation of communication, as far as I am currently concerned, is that of "respect". Respect is the basic ingredient with which every human being, of whatever age or state, has the right to be treated. This is of course a two way process. One cannot expect to be respected or treated with respect, unless one accords the same to others. However, I do appreciate that this is not always as easy to do, as one would hope. This is the case, whether dealing with young or old whether one is well or has some form of illness.

Unless an individual knows you well or knows about your current state, whatever that might be, there is the likelihood that their respect for you may be jeopardised by your statements, actions, or reactions, to them and / or situations in which they are involved with you. These may be social, professional contacts, or as members of the public in the course of day to day contacts. These reactions may be viewed as understandable / reasonable. However, they do still pose difficulties in respect of their effect on the degree of trust that one has in others and they in you. This in turn may affect the future quality of relationship and communication between the persons concerned.

Dementia adds an additional aspect of potential risk to the breakdown of respect between dementi and others. Its associated behavioural and social issues may understandably lead to false opinions / assumptions regarding the person concerned. They may be considered to be less desirable, than previously, in social gatherings and often induce a perceived, if not real, patronising response from others. One has to admit, that this response is not surprising and probably not unreasonable. However, it does pose a serious risk to one's confidence and self-respect. This, in turn, risks a desire for the protection of increased isolation. I suspect that this scenario applies just as much in the day-care or residential care settings, as it does for individuals still living in the community.

So, what is the solution to the issues I raise in this blog. Firstly, I do not think there is a "one fits all" solution. The situation is complex, as are the responses and interactions between all parties involved. However, on further reflection, it certainly could help, if people like myself, with dementia, made as great an effort as possible, while we are still able, to behave in such a way that the frequency of occurrence of these problems are minimised. In addition, it could also be helpful, if the general public, carers, both formal and informal, health care professionals and social care professionals were better educated in aspects of this topic. This could then lead to a greater understanding of the benefits to all concerned of the importance and significance of "respect".

JSAFGA Posted by A GOOD LIFE WITH DEMENTIA at 10:57

SUNDAY, 20 NOVEMBER 2011

FOG THE LEVELLER

This morning's early morning walk down the valley in thick fog, ironically, proved to be another opportunity for a degree of possible alternative enlightenment and reflection.

Firstly, ahead of me I noticed that Blossom, my Springer Spaniel, had lay down in a submissive manner on the ground. I then noticed in the mists, what appeared to be the outline of a large cow. In the normal way, Blossom would not react in this manner, at the sight of a cow. She is familiar with the local cattle, as are they with her and their presence never upset the other. However, as I got within 20 yards of the shape, I could make out the outline, not of a cow, but of two men and a couple of dogs, hence, my own dog staying laid down. The people concerned had waited, as they had obviously seen my figure looming out of the fog as I approached and they too were not sure as to whether or not I was an approaching beast. When we all came within distance of positive sighting and identification of each other, noting all was well, we exchanged greetings and carried on our respective travels.

The above event reminded me that, there are occasions when clarity of thought and speech are being joined by others in whose company I am present, while at the same time, I have become conscious that I am struggling with aspects of fogginess of thought and communication. However, this morning's fog provided what I considered was a "level playing field" for all concerned. The other two people present and their dogs, were just as unsure and unclear as me and Blossom. They were evidently reassured when Blossom came with me up the other side of the valley. I sat for a while in the fog and felt a strange degree of satisfaction that those two people had briefly experienced an aspect of the practical reality of the lack of internal clarity and the fogginess similar to which I regularly experience, even on sunny days.

One cannot reasonably expect, empathy and understanding of one's confusion, memory loss and episodes of frustrated verbal aggression. One certainly doesn't want sympathy, as that does NOT help at all. However, in the quiet safety of this blog, I am able to give external expression, which I find helpful, to some internal analysis of my onward journey through what is in general a "Good Life With Dementia".

JSAFGA Posted by A GOOD LIFE WITH DEMENTIA at 06:16

TUESDAY, 22 NOVEMBER 2011

A TRICKY WINDY PATH

Here we go again, an expression of thoughts and inner feelings / emotions that are around on a daily basis. Some more pronounced than others, on days in question, dependent upon the circumstances. It is a tricky, winding path this journey is currently following. Moments of great fun, laughter and joy. Others of bitter frustration and anger when misunderstood, ignored, or intentionally avoided and side-lined. Those one or two who avoid me, I think, mainly do so out of a feared concern regarding their lack of ability to cope with / handle my possible response to them. There is a wealth of misunderstanding, some no doubt on my part, which I suppose is understandable, in relation to the manner of social communication with the likes of myself, at this stage of the dementia journey. Fortunately, my wife and carer understand my current need for simplicity and straight talking when dealing with others. Unfortunately, not everyone else can.

The above may seem a bit of a self-centred approach / rant. It is to a certain extent, yet this perceived need for simple straight forward communication is a NEED, to minimise confusion. Confusion leads to frustration and misunderstanding and the consequence of this sometimes leads to others being offended by my reaction.

I hope that any fellow travellers on this journey, be they carers or fellow dementiates, who may read this blog, get some comfort from knowing that, if they are experiencing these irritations or the consequences of the same, they are not travelling alone!

JSAFGA Posted by A GOOD LIFE WITH DEMENTIA at 10:46

THURSDAY, 24 NOVEMBER 2011

TAKE THE RISK HAVE YOUR VOICE HEARD

On a good day and when necessary, I seek to take opportunities to take charge of events either at home or in the company of others, including suggestion of solutions to problematic situations. My wife has increasingly supported me in doing so, in the four years since I was diagnosed.

Now, of course, sometimes the above can be tricky. One has to try to be sure that you have totally understood the situation, before proffering one's guidance. However, for an increased degree of personal respect / credence, I believe it a risk worth taking. In these situations, I hope that I have not misunderstood what has been said or misread the situation. There again, don't non dementing people, frequently, do that? Of course, they do!

So I say to my fellow dementing brothers and sisters, have courage, speak out when you think it appropriate, offer advice and a view, when you think it is warranted. You may get a worried look or bemused response from acquaintances who think they know you, but really don't. However, let them have their own moment of confusion to deal with, we have enough of our own! In that golden moment of clear thinking be brave, seize the opportunity, make the statement, offer the advice, demonstrate your knowledge and understanding of the situation, whatever it might be.

Take the opportunity to build up / repair any damaged self-worth, or lost confidence. Let others see the positive aspect of your hidden depths, dispel for some the myth that, having dementia means that you do not, anymore, have the potential to provide a degree of leadership, insight and understanding. Take the risk!

JSAFGA Posted by A GOOD LIFE WITH DEMENTIA at 10:34

MONDAY, 28 NOVEMBER 2011

A HELPFUL TECHNIQUE

I share with you a technique that I find helpful, particularly when having difficulty remembering someone's name during a conversation. Not necessarily the name of the person to whom I am speaking, but usually the name of someone else to whom I wish to refer. This technique is probably more easily adopted in a small village community of about 100 people, like that where I live, rather than in a town. However, even there, it may have its uses for communicating about a person who lives in the same road or vicinity.

What I do, in instances when I cannot recall the name of someone about whom I want to refer during a conversation, is I may refer to their trade. For example, I will sometimes refer to the farmer who lives in the farmhouse at the top of the lane on the bend. The person to whom I am speaking will invariably know who I mean and will refer to them by their name. This allows the conversation to continue, fairly, unimpeded. Once the individual with whom I am conversing has understood that sometimes they will be required to provide reminder links of this nature, all is well for both parties. It comes as a bit of a shock for them on the first couple of occasions, but from then on, they are usually happy to oblige in this manner. The initial shock for the other party is when they know that you know the other individual well, to whom you are referring and whose name you cannot remember. They therefore wonder why you are communicating in this form of descriptive manner. On the second occasion, I usually come clean and state that I sometimes have memory recall difficulties. This I find the simplest and most straightforward approach and the least stressful for all concerned. It is like anything else, once one knows the extent of a problem then one can easier deal with it.

JSAFGA Posted by A GOOD LIFE WITH DEMENTIA at 13:00

TUESDAY, 6 DECEMBER 2011

EMOTIONAL DIMENSIONS

Today, I am minded that our friend dementia is the bearer of the gift of exaggerated emotion.

As we are now well and truly in the run up to Christmas and more than halfway through Advent, the season of emotional highs and lows advances at a rapid rate. The coming together of family and friends at different stages of the Christmas season, is one to be viewed with a mixture of emotional value including Bon Ami and greetings of exaggerated depth. Of course, this is balanced by genuine expressions of love, warmth and hospitality between givers and receivers. So, I ask myself what is my problem with it all? I say my problem, as I acknowledge that like so many issues that annoy or result in an adverse reaction from me these days, my reaction to others, cannot in general be blamed on them, but rather, how I now respond to them.

In a similar manner to the exaggerated emotional festive responses referred to above, I find the ability to assimilate and accept the in genuine aspects, far more difficult to tolerate, than previously. I succumb more readily now to taking the less understanding and benevolent approach to such individuals and situations. Why this, one is may reasonably ask? I think it is associated with my now perceived necessity and therefore efforts, to minimise confusion, by increasingly needing to focus on what I consider to be reality. A more black and white approach to relationships, I now find easier to deal with. This of course conflicts with the complexity of normal human personality and relationships. These of course require great flexibility and understanding of persons and situations, in order to maintain stability and the avoidance of misunderstandings. However, this of itself is conflictual from my perspective, if confusion is to be reduced.

I am, today, further minded that dementia appears to lead to exaggeration of certain pre-existing psychological /emotional facets. Just as Christmas often leads to heightened emotional states, I am conscious that a number of my own personality traits are also being increased with intensity as time progresses. It is possible therefore, that dementia has a particular facet that not only diminishes things like memory, but also extends /exaggerates some pre-existing traits. For example, a person like myself with a generally outgoing personality, on occasions, finds that, in certain situations, the gregarious nature pervades even more than it did of old. The extension of these boundaries, beyond their previous limits, can be problematical not only for myself, but more importantly for others in whose company I am present. So far, no lasting damage has been done, as far as I am aware! However, this is obviously an extra burden for my wife, my carer, to have to cope with, less about the recipient.

Another example of the above, where the exaggerated personality trait being increasingly heightened, in a similar manner, is that of straight talking, "calling a spade a spade and not a dustpan"! This increase has led to a diminution of my diplomacy and tact. Now, what needs to be understood by the reader is that this is not an intentional act and it is often only when someone expresses their concern or hurt, that one sometimes accepts or understands that one has overstepped an acceptable boundary line. Even though at the time it did not seem to be the case.

NB. In view of the above, is it any wonder that we are eventually admitted to specialised residential care?!! It takes an enormous amount of love, care, persistence, determination and understanding, on the part of our carer, to cope with the increasing complexity of the challenges we present.

My final thought for this blog is that, as Christmas approaches, we dementiates should look forward to enjoying as many aspects of the season as possible, firmly in the knowledge, that in spite of our varying degrees of eccentricity, there is an enormous amount of Love, Good Will and Understanding around us.

JSAFGA Posted by A GOOD LIFE WITH DEMENTIA at 07:34

SUNDAY, 11 DECEMBER 2011

KEEP IT SIMPLE

With Christmas fast approaching and the complexity of emotional strains, the happiness and sadness that we allow it to bring, my increasing view is Keep it Simple. In these times of financial austerity, this may be a blessing for many that they have no option but to keep it simple in respect of being able / unable to purchase gifts. There may, ultimately, be a long-term advantageous spin off to this enforced necessity for many, to rein in the personal expenditure this year. Often the simplest gifts are the most cherished. The small uncomplicated gift from a child, often has the greater impact and meaning than some luxurious gift from a wealthy friend or family member.

Now, you may ask where this blog is going. Is it his personal soap box version of a church sermon? Well no, it is not meant to be that, even though it is being written on a Sunday evening! I am minded of the simplicity angle as I am, increasingly, finding that as the months pass I the complexity of issues and situations best avoided, in order to maintain clarity of thought and understanding. The adoption of a simple approach and the association with simplicity is not born from any high moralistic ideal, akin to a monastic existence. Rather it is driven by the wish to be able to function normally as possible, to try to avoid detection, by the newly met or the stranger, of being a card-carrying member of the dementia club! Not that I am ashamed of membership, but rather, that I wish to keep as many aspects of life, relationships and thought processes, as simple as possible.

JSAFGA Posted by A GOOD LIFE WITH DEMENTIA at 10:27

FRIDAY, 16 DECEMBER 2011

REPORT ON DEMENTIA CARE IN ACUTE HOSPITAL WARDS

Today, a report from the Royal College of Psychiatrists in the UK, expressed concern regarding the provision of care Dementia patients receive, in acute medical and surgical wards, when admitted for treatment of other clinical conditions. It states that, staff in these clinical areas do not currently provide an acceptable level of appropriate care for Dementia patients. A number of stated reasons for this include the lack of appropriate training.

To improve the above apparently deteriorating situation, I would suggest that all staff involved in clinical care, as part of their formal clinical training, should be required to demonstrate their personal ability in the following areas, before being granted their formal post-graduate clinical / medical professional qualification:-

a. A CARING NATURE
b. EMPATHETIC ABILITY
c. UNDERSTANDING OF THE SIGNIFICANCE OF RESPECT AND PERSONAL DIGNITY
d. HIGH LEVELS OF INTERPERSONAL COMMUNICATION SKILLS
e. A SENSE OF HUMOUR

The above list is not comprehensive. However, I believe that anyone who is going to be considered fit to provide clinical care for any person, whether being treated in the community or in hospital, should, as a minimum requirement, be required to demonstrate a high degree of personal skills and ability in the above areas, in addition to their clinical /medical knowledge. If adopted, this requirement would not require any significant increase in financial cost to the education of potential health practitioners. However, the potential outcome in respect of improvement in the quality of patient care could be significant.

JSAFGA Posted by A GOOD LIFE WITH DEMENTIA at 14:21

WEDNESDAY, 21 DECEMBER 2011

MEMORIES

Christmastide invariably has the effect of summoning up memories, both good and not so good, for most people. It affords a time, amidst the hustle and bustle, if only briefly, to remember times and people from both our present and past life. For some, this can be as traumatic as it can be enjoyable for others, dependent on their individual life's journey so far.

I am increasingly finding that, even though my short-term memory retention is gradually diminishing, the long-term memory of events, places and people from times long past, is increasingly active. Now the other interesting and beneficial aspect is that the clarity of things pleasant from the past is the main focus and the few unpleasant experiences have gradually dissipated, to the same degree that ability to recall the positive and enjoyable times and relationships has increased. Whether this is purely as a result of my particular positive psychological makeup and attitude to life, I do not know. Maybe it is something that the majority of Dementees experience - interesting research project for some clinician maybe?!

The above, is a positive aspect of the disease as far as I am concerned. If clarity of memory thought is, generally, only available to the positive aspects of one's past life, then this will help one, as far as possible, to maintain "A Good Life With Dementia".

In case I am not moved to write another blog before Christmas, I would like to wish any readers, wherever you live, a Happy Christmas and New Year. To the followers in Russia, a Happy New Year and celebration of Christmas in January.

To all Carers and fellow Dementors, Peace and Love.

JSAFGA Posted by A GOOD LIFE WITH DEMENTIA at 08:47

WEDNESDAY, 28 DECEMBER 2011

THOUGHTS AS THE NEW YEAR APPROACHES

Another New Year approaches this coming weekend. What does it have in store for all of us. Personally, I do not look forward to it in trepidation or with a sense of either elation or expectation. I find, even more so these days, to be able, in my head, to be prepared to experience the unexpected. I have no use for planning too far ahead or creating unnecessary expectations of oneself or of others. A life of unrealistic expectations will only disappoint and frustrate. One must not have unrealistic expectations of oneself, nor for that matter, of others understanding of you. One cannot have a full understanding of how, when or where the dementing journey will lead, or the pace at which significant milestones will be reached. This need not be disconcerting, if one is able and prepared to "go with the flow". To follow this approach may help avoid or at least reduce the personal impact on reaching different stages of the condition's progress.

Having said the above, while at one level I believe the above laid-back approach applies to myself, there are in fact major contradictions in reality. If I am so philosophical and calm about future events etc, then why does the slightest alteration to arrangements on a day to day basis seem to agitate me so. Interestingly, I find these relatively minor adaptations difficult to handle. I find, increasingly, I rely on the certainty, reliability and concreteness of arrangements and what people say. A black and white, certain, approach to matters, I find far more reassuring and easier to cope with, than more flexible arrangements. I have an increasing need and expectancy of individuals to say what they mean and therefore to mean what they say. Elements of social niceties, I find, increasingly, difficult to maintain. These relate mainly to responding to what other individuals may have said. For example, if I suspect someone has said something for effect, rather than what they truly mean / believe, then I find it difficult not to say so.

My immediate family, including my young adult grandchildren, have adapted magnificently to the slight and in some cases the apparently discernible personality changes that have taken place in the past few years. This a source of great comfort, knowing that I can continue to be totally relaxed and be myself in their company. This has been particularly important during the recent festive period.

HAPPY 2012

JSAFGA Posted by A GOOD LIFE WITH DEMENTIA at 11:02

FRIDAY, 30 DECEMBER 2011

EXPRESSING YOUR THOUGHTS and SEEKING CLARIFICATION

The release and freedom that expressing one's thoughts can have, I find is extremely beneficial. Don't worry if some of the recipients think you're a bit "off the wall". At the end of the day, it is better to do so, rather than bottling up the thoughts / emotions/ confusion, as this can quickly lead only to frustration and resentment. This applies to both non dementees, as well as members of the dementia club. No doubt the non dementiates will find a more diplomatic manner in which to do this, than I do. However, the end result will I am sure be just as beneficial. I find it interesting that, nowadays, if someone is equally obnoxious to me as, apparently, I may have been to them, it does not create a major issue as far as I am concerned. I appreciate and value, what I view, as their honesty. Tact and diplomacy are further down my pecking order of importance, these days, than openness and honesty of thought and view.

I suppose this notable change in approach, may once again, be a tactic to minimise the risk of confusion. While previously, the complexity and diversity of others psychological influences on their approach to verbal communication, I always found stimulating and interesting. However, this is no longer the case. I now have a tendency to insist that people say what they mean and therefore mean what they say. The literal meaning of what is said is of far more significance and importance to me in verbal communication, than previously. The mental stimulation formally gained from unravelling the "music behind the words", no longer stimulates, it now only tends to frustrate.

I became acutely aware of the above, once again, in a social setting, while having dinner with friends in their home yesterday evening. I found that on a number of occasions, a throw away remark by one of the other guests would prompt my request for clarification of exactly what it was they meant. After a number of such instances, the fellow guest started to indicate their frustration at my requesting that they clarify what it was precisely they were saying and the point they were making. The person concerned is someone who knows me quite well and of the issues I have in relation to verbal communication and understanding. However, in this setting, they obviously found it more difficult to cope with these requests for clarification. On the one hand, I understand their frustration, on the other, unless clarification is sort when required, the misunderstandings that arise may have far worse consequences.

It is occasions like that mentioned above, that can tend lead one to seek further isolation in one's own company, as a more satisfactory option, rather than maintaining the already reducing social circle. However, the risks and consequences of cutting oneself off further, socially, not only for the dementee but, as importantly, for my wife and carer, are equally unsatisfactory.

It may be that this is a phenomenon shared by other fellow dementees? If so, then to any carers, be they health professionals, or relatives, I suggest that, if you find the dementee you are looking after, has, or starts with the above tendencies, then it may be for the same reasons that I have identified in my own case.

Tomorrow is New Year's Eve and my wife and I are going to see in the New Year with four other trusted and understanding friends, who are happy with "straight talking", so it should be a trouble free start to 2012!

A happy and healthy 2012 is wished for any readers of this blog - thank you for sharing in my "Good Life With Dementia".

JSAFGA Posted by A GOOD LIFE WITH DEMENTIA at 09:26

FRIDAY, 3 FEBRUARY 2012

UNCERTAIN TIMES

Uncertain times at the moment - Not sure what to think or do. Motivation waning slightly. Might be the time of the year. Slight loss of motivation and enthusiasm. Hopefully this will pass. Still thinking positively although the future does not seem as bright as previously. Slightly demotivated - not inclined to play the guitar for past few months. Still thinking positives thoughts and general health is still good. Still making sure the daily walks happen and enjoying the blue skies and the frost. The outdoors and hillside a great blessing. Intend to keep looking on the bright side - have got so much to be grateful and thankful for. Got to be able to take the rough with the smooth us problem solvers. The snow drops look beautiful in the lane. The dementia journey is a challenging one yet life is still Good.

JSAFGA Posted by A GOOD LIFE WITH DEMENTIA at 06:44

WEDNESDAY, 15 FEBRUARY 2012

YOU ARE STILL WHO YOU WERE

It is easy to become disillusioned by the fact that, due to the dementing process, one is aware that one is not as one was, and also therefore that this will no doubt be apparent to others. This may specifically apply to those who have known you for a number of years. The differences may not be too significant or discernible to others. To some, the changes they may seemed marked. Your nearest and dearest will be the ones who have experienced and will be most aware of the gradual changes that are and have taken place over the years and months. Those who did not know the old you, will therefore be non the wiser and it is easier for them to accept you as you are, as they have no reference point from the past with which to compare.

The relevance of the above is that, I believe, we dementees should remain cognisant of the following - Although subtle and sometimes not so subtle changes are taking place, both in relation to how we are and how we are perceived by others, nevertheless, it is a fact that "You Are Still Who You Were". I mention this, as it occurs to me that, although on occasions, recent events may be difficult to recall, and behavioural issues may not be perceived to be like "the old you". The fact is that, the You are still You, the combination of, the You of the past and the You of today. These will combine to be an integral part of the you of tomorrow. To retain this view, I find helpful, as an aid to maintaining an essential degree of self-esteem, that dementia has the potential to undermine.

JSAFGA Posted by A GOOD LIFE WITH DEMENTIA at 07:43

FRIDAY, 17 FEBRUARY 2012

NB. MISSING BLOGS

I realise that I have posted 5 of 2012 blogs on another blog page of mine that has the same name, i.e. "A Good Life With Dementia". I had unwittingly created that site when setting up the original one. I will endeavour to ensure that all future blogs are published on the one site, namely this one! Sorry about the slip up!

JSAFGA Posted by A GOOD LIFE WITH DEMENTIA at 07:31

FRIDAY, 17 FEBRUARY 2012

MISSING LINKS

I feel disposed to write about "Missing Links" as this can be an occupational hazard / challenge on the road of the "Good Life". Missing links can be frustrating for everyone in all walks of life and at all stages of life. They often eventually reveal themselves sooner or later. Even when they don't, their relevance has usually passed, as has their significance.

Now, what are the sort of links that go missing? They can be many and varied, sometimes words, sometimes ideas, sometimes thought processes, sometimes emotions, sometimes relating to memories. The fact that the link goes missing, whether temporarily or long term, can cause a moment or two or even longer, of disruption / consternation. However, it is important to try and adapt as quickly as possible to the new situation, without the unrecalled, yet real, link that is missing.

Sometimes, although a thought process is interrupted, due to a missing link, it is possible that this may be advantageous, provided that the frustration associated with it can be quickly overcome. The potential advantage is that the brain has to devise another strategy for dealing with this newfound situation. It helps, if one can get oneself into a long-term positive mindset. This then ensures that every set back, while being acknowledged as such, is still seen as an opportunity, to draw on the hidden resources that the brain and one's personality can muster. This positive attitude, if able to be adopted, will help to overcome the disadvantage of no longer having the "Missing Links".

JSAFGA Posted by A GOOD LIFE WITH DEMENTIA at 08:12

MONDAY, 20 FEBRUARY 2012

VALLEYS AND HILLSIDES

This morning when walking with the dog, viewing the surrounding hills and valleys, the thoughts that enjoined me were that, from on high and looking down over it all, it resembled many a person's life path. The compartmentalised fields divided by the limestone walls, the deep valleys, the deserted and dilapidated stone barns which once gave shelter and warmth to both cattle, sheep and farmer, many now near collapsed, due to years of neglect and the ravages of the weather. These places hold countless memories for and of, many people over centuries. Those people were real, as were the livestock they looked after. Not only the people who worked the land, but also the many thousands of walkers and visitors who have visited the area.

The patch quilted scenery, like life, contains many seasonal changing aspects and yet also the steadfastness of the main physical features. The river, whose waters disappear into the underground limestone caverns during the summer and then reappear during the autumn rains and winter's snow. To be able contemplate these things is a wondrous aspect of this life journey. To be able to peacefully reflect on such things brings a great joy. This far exceeds the benefits of being able to remember every happening of the day or everything that has to be done. The frustrations and annoyance, due to lack of understanding, confusions and memory loss, verbal fluency etc, fade into insignificance as silent witness of the depth and beauty of lives past and present and creation are contemplated, helps to make journeying this way a "Good Life With Dementia"!

JSAFGA. Posted by [A GOOD LIFE WITH DEMENTIA](#) at [08:28](#)

MONDAY, 5 MARCH 2012

RAISING OTHER'S SPIRITS CAN HELP MAINTAIN YOUR OWN

Some days are better than others, sometimes our spirit's are uplifted for a variety of reasons. Sometimes only a relatively small occurrence can set us back. To occasionally focus on our own particular situation can be healthy, as part of a reality check. However, I find it helpful not to linger too long, on the variety of relatively minor enforced amendments to life, as a result of one's condition. As with everyone too much introspection can distract from the opportunities one still has to brighten one's own and other's days and to help lighten their burden. Our carer is the one most deserving of this support.

To be seen to be having a positive approach to life, can be uplifting to others, as well as oneself and can be a positive boost to the one shouldering the main responsibility for our care. With the resulting positivity, high spirits and the associated tendency, nowadays, for the mouth to engage before the brain, my approach is to go with the flow. Although sometimes this may result in slight alienation or cause raised eyebrows among a few, on balance, the benefits to both oneself and one's loved one, outweighs any resulting negativity from others.

To try and stay positive, is the least one can do for both ourselves and those who care for us. When the occasion arises that the negative aspects come into focus, we are better equipped to minimise their impact. We can then continue journeying on our "good life with dementia".

JSAFGA Posted by A GOOD LIFE WITH DEMENTIA at 12:02

FRIDAY, 16 MARCH 2012

SPRING BRINGS NEW OPPORTUNITIES

The arrival of Spring brings new opportunities for a fresh approach to life, as well as to living. For those of us who are lucky to be fit enough to be able to enjoy the first few weeks of the new season, we can enjoy the removal of the dead Winter growth revealing new plant life. The daffodils formed flowers getting ready to open, as are the buds on many bushes and trees. All that is required now is a small amount of warm sunshine. The new growth bursting forth, may also raise our spirits. We can look forward to the commencement of the eagerly awaited colourful show. We can shake off the gloom of Winter and make another new start. A change in activities can also help give one a new outlook on life in general. A change in outlook, whatever one's state, may help one better cope with one's situation and enhance one's ability to maximise their potential to enjoy the many differing opportunities life has to offer.

JSAFGA Posted by A GOOD LIFE WITH DEMENTIA at 14:03

SUNDAY, 18 MARCH 2012

RIDING THE WAVES

It might be considered by some, that way to deal with the daily issues associated with dementia, would be to strive to fight for the lost moments of memory or thought. This maybe a satisfactory approach for some. However, my experience to date, I say to date because it is the only day with which we have to deal. is While making sure that each day has some moments of significant action, be that physical and / or mental stimulation, I do not find it helpful or consider it wise, to start struggling with temporary lapses of memory or mood.

In the periods, like those referred to above, I find it best to ride the wave, of whatever the circumstance might be. Like all waves, they usually start small with a gradually increasing swell, then before long, break and dissipate. They can either be allowed to swamp the craft, or alternatively, if it is steered in a skilful manner, the wave will carry boat forward safely.

One is the skipper of one's own craft and the journey can be a good, provided one uses the rough water to carry you forward rather drown you.

JSAFGA Posted by A GOOD LIFE WITH DEMENTIA at 08:45

MONDAY, 2 APRIL 2012

SENIOR MOMENTS

Yesterday was one of more "senior moments" than usual. Being Palm Sunday the early morning walk with Blossom (my dog) over the meadows commenced at 9am with a view to being back home by 10.30am to walk up the road to the village church for the 11am Palm Sunday service. However, where or how I know not, but the time flew by, somehow unnoticed. Relaxing and thoughts scudding by like the clouds as we went from field to field. Hare and pheasant being sprung by Bloss and I enjoying the sporting chases. No bloodshed and everyone creature exercised and stimulated by the occasion. It wasn't till arriving back home at 11.30am that I realised some time had passed unaccounted for. Still it was a most enjoyable walk and I was able eventually to catch up with the palm and donkey procession around the village in time for the final reading and hymn, followed by the soup and cheese in the village hall.

These moments in time come and go, some we remember some we don't - be not concerned - all is well.

JSAFGA Posted by A GOOD LIFE WITH DEMENTIA at 12:11

THURSDAY, 26 APRIL 2012

RISKING EMBARRASSMENT

While never wishing to offend, I increasingly find, nowadays, that in order to maintain courage in my ability to retain mental independence, discretion has to occasionally be sacrificed. Risks are now more frequently taken in relation to verbal communication with others. This, I think, is possibly due to the combination of both trying to continue to demonstrate that one still has the ability to maintain independent logical thought processes and also meeting the need to demonstrate to others that one still has a degree of ability, wit, knowledge and wisdom, to hold one's own, if sometimes only briefly, in discussion. To satisfy the need to prove to oneself and others, that one is not yet "yesterday's man", is vital. To make one's point, or explain oneself, or to fully comprehend what another is saying, it is sometimes necessary to insist on frequently recapping what has been said. This may prove to be annoying / frustrating, even confusing, for the other party, particularly if they do not know you. However, the risk of upsetting them or even causing embarrassment, I consider is one worth taking.

JSAFGA Posted by A GOOD LIFE WITH DEMENTIA at 12:48

A COLLECTION OF POEMS

By Joe Ashton

2011

THE DAYS THEY ARE A CHANGING

The summer's long and balmy days, gently, give way to less tranquil ways. A mist now into the valley descends to announce the arrival of cooling trends. The early morning dews foretell the oncoming whitened fingers of the frost. The strengthening breeze and billowing clouds hint at balmy times being lost

Swallows, Martins and Starlings make last minute preparations for journeys south. Meals of insects and flies, of various kinds are now foremost on their minds. That extra layer of essential flesh and feather, will see them through all weather. Land and seas are to be crossed before alighting in the warmer climes away from frost.

Berries aplenty have been seen to form, to help keep animal, bird and mankind warm. Their colours bright and shiny, attract us from afar and also help fill many a jam jar. Animals feed, with intent, a few weeks more, until shelter they seek with a Winter store. Indoor accommodation is sought by mouse and rat, but care is needed to avoid the cat.

Fox, a mate, he seeks soon and sings to his betrothed beneath the harvest moon. A union they will be a fixin, then in spring cubs will be the gift from his Vixen. Badgers are busy finding worms, grubs and other fayre, to get a thicker fatty layer. That extra coat will be needed, if their winter hibernation is to be unimpeded.

The final cut of silage now in store, not till next July will there be more. Cattle, not long on the pastures grazing, soon in Winter quarters they will be lazing. Calves continue to be born, although in the hay filled sheds to keep warm. Not a bad place to stay, good enough for Jesus anyway.

The clouds, with ever changing shape, shower rain on the meadow walker's cape. It won't be long before these droplets turn to hail, warning of future snows travail. Before those cold winter days arrive, we can still enjoy the

Joe Ashton

beauty of the sky. Glorious colours of leaf's early autumn show, provide a warming inward glow.

The Seasons, Days and Life are a changin yay, lets enjoy the beauty of each day. Family and friends, like the seasons, come and go. So enjoy each day, a gift from God, whether, wind, hail, rain, or snow. In the changes, however great or small they may be, is a message for you and me.

September 2011

AUTUMN MUSES IN THE HILLS

The greens of summer gradually fade and the leaves to the carpeted ground are laid
Spectacular colours start to shew, the lowering sun adding to the hew
A scampering hare, in full flight, chasing home before the night
Escapes the fox's early hunting spree, as Ms Reynaud stirs under his tree
The late swoops of hawk and kite spell the oncoming of the night A late foray down to grass, gorse and bracken they, to snatch the final meal of the day
Badgers, foraging for worms and berries go, before onset of winter's snow
Their strength and fat reserves must build, to survive the icy blasts, with bellies filled
Cows to wintering sheds will soon be led, stalls filled with straw for their bed
Feed to them will now to be given, while inside they lie, till warm spring sun fills the sky
The beef cattle on the meadows still roam, yet they too, in winter, have an indoor home
These hardy stalwarts of the range can cope with nature's every change
Tups by sheep are now feted and the paint on yew's rear proves love consummated
Lambs will be born in early spring, no matter what the ravages winters' fling
Feathered friends have gone to warmer climes, only local birds hear the church chimes
Those visitors will return again in spring, as will human walkers country visiting
Mole, squirrel and vole plus the stoat, an ermine stole made from its winter coat Are all very active now, with many a pheasant and partridge on the bough
Winds north, south, east and west, what clothes to wear for the best?
The sky one moment brilliant blue, next, darkest grey, no more the view
A reflection of life's cycle God's seasons bring, till we enter that Heavenly Spring.

PREPARING FOR CHRISTMAS

Now Halloween and Bon Fire Night have gone, it's time for Santa to get his skates on
Letters coming in from children far and wide asking for dolls and ponies and even a slide
Requests for toys of all shapes and sizes, books, computer games and doll's houses
Footballs and Teddies that will fit in the pocket, and the latest today, was for a rocket!

Santa's helpers are hard at work, to get the job done they will not shirk
No matter how late that letter to Santa is written, he will be able to bring that kitten
He greatly loves this time of year, to hear the bells and folk of good cheer

The reindeer are growing their warm winter coats, to stay cosy in the air, as they float
The sleigh they pull is being painted red, although you will not see it, as it fly's overhead
The storage cupboards have been given a clean, and not a speck of dust can now be seen

A miracle Santa can get all the toys, on board his sleigh, for the world's girls & boys
He doesn't't need a plane, train, car or van because he is God's special Christmas man
Soon he will be ironing his smart red suit, while one of his friends will polish his boots

To spread some happiness, is Santa's mission each day, and so let's help him on his way
Get out a paper and pen, to drop him a line, or even email him, that will be fine
He's delighted to hear from you, now winters near, or even at any other time of the year

Don't worry, he won't mind, whatever you ask, for God's Santa there is no, too big a task

A reminder to everyone BIG and small, that the time is approaching to give Santa a call

He will bring the gifts that you request, but make sure he knows the one you want best

8th November 2011

TALE OF TODAY'S AUTUMN SOJOURN (ADULTS AND YOUNG ADULTS ONLY)

I share with you this tale, a TRUE one at that, involving a walk with Bloss, a hen and a cat
To Alstonfield, Bloss and I went today, a journey of six miles return, over the meadow's way.

Deer stalker hat, muddy green wellies and shooting stick, we started off at quite a lick.
Through fields and stiles we went alone, only radio2 playing through the I Phone.
A glorious walk, no fog today, striding along without delay.
An occasional seat upon the stick, before arrival at "The George" pub in good nick.
Passing sheep and cattle without a fuss, this mode of travel beats the bus.
Up the hill, no lift to hitch, we enter the village via cricket pitch.
Down the lane and past the old forge, around the corner and we are at "The George"
Blossom is tied to the base of a table bench, while I go look for a serving wench
The landlady soon does our order take, an Irish Coffee and ham sandwich, my favourite, make no mistake. Your welcome inside, with the dog she says, but I decline the offer, knowing the odd behaviour of humans these days.

The Irish Coffee and sandwich gone down a treat, it was once more, time to get on our feet
We retraced our route to the cricket pitch, Bloss on a lead to avoid any hitch.
As we neared the gate, she spied a cat, who scarpered quick to avoid a spat.
Bloss includes cats, rats and birds in her list of fair game, the pheasant, ducks, rabbits and hare, there all there by name. Meanwhile the cat had entered a copse full of hens, where plenty of mice and rats have their dens. We pass through a stile on to the cricket pitch, heading off homeward, once more crossing a ditch

At this stage I think it now safe to believe, my girl off the lead, no trouble will heed

Oh dear, this is not the case, as immediately back to the hens and cat she did chase
Over the wall into the copse she did leap high, to get the cat who given her the evil eye
Apparently, the cat was nowhere to be seen, but a number of hens running and squawking and clucking was the theme. I arrived and alighted over the gate, scattering frightened fowl - but it was too late! The hens are no match for a Bloss on the chase and one fowl, oh heck! was downed with a clean snap of the neck.

No feathers flying or blood to spill, no sign of trauma around the bill
An almighty shout from me to the Bloss, she dropped the bird and awaited the boss
A reprimand having been made amid the consternation, now restitution had to be a consideration. Should we high tail it over the hills, with a fox to be blamed for the ills, or find the owner and pay the bill. The latter we decided should be the way, then we could return for more Irish Coffee someday. An elderly lady was spotted through an adjoining cottage with a towel- she was the owner of the fowl. A straight and open confession of the crime we did make, with humble apologies for our mistake.

"That was my favourite hen" the lady said, when she heard that it was dead
One might have known that would be the case, when compensation was offered as a means of saving face
A sum of fifteen quid was the stated replacement cost, for the old broiler that was lost
We traversed back home, oer valley and hill, the hen's demise not spoiling the thrill

Tomorrow these steps I will retrace, money in hand, as a saving grace.
The Bloss will have to miss this trip, although with another Irish coffee, a toast to her good health I will sip.

23rd November 2011

ADVENT

Advent has an exciting ring, as we prepare to welcome our King
Yes Christ, the visitor for whom we prepare, opted to join us in stable bare
Mary and Joseph to Bethlehem came, via mountain path and stony lane
Their infant, son, before the dawn, in that humble dwelling would be born

They did not know God's true intent, having nothing but Faith to remain content
Faith, the greatest gift of all, still brings us through the cruelest squall
The infant babe, a gift from above, brought Joy and Peace and Hope and Love
So again, as before, we prepare for Christmas, as in days of yore

With Joy and Hope and Peace and Love, God's Son came from Heaven above
No flitting phase or recent trend, his message lasts until the end
Enjoy the God given life you have, through fun and sadness, raise a laugh
The Joy, Peace and Love the Saviour brings overcomes all troublesome things

Try, keeping Faith in God, with Joy and Fun and as with Santa, His gifts will come
For all Mankind, God sent His Son, a friend and protector for everyone
And even if you cannot believe, doesn't worry, He will still be with you on Christmas Eve.

23rd November 2011

STILL HE SLEPT

The ox and ass bayed, a newborn babe in their manger laid - still He slept
Shepherds with sheep, an angel announced, an appointment to keep - still He slept
Three wise men to the stable came, to see the babe, Jesus by name - still He slept
Gold, frankincense and myrrh they brought, fit for a king, they thought - still He slept
Innkeeper called; "what's the fuss?", on the arrival of the One to save us - still He slept
Alleluias sung, with joy and mirth, to celebrate our Saviour's birth - still He slept
Herod wished this babe to kill, so through desert flight the family mill - still He slept
Of Man born, the Son of God, a human gift from the Lord above - still He slept
When in life, sometimes forlorn, think of Galilee, that storm where - still He slept
This Son of God, born of Man, suffered fears and doubts, as we all can - still He slept
His Father's work, He would see through, to save the likes of me and you - still He slept
Through Faith, Peace and Love, a joyful message from above - still He slept
God's Love of us All, is a promise kept, so 'tis no wonder - still He slept

Dad's (Grandpa / Great Grandpa's birthday tomorrow 9th December RIP)

December 8th, 2011

SPIRITS OF CHRISTMAS

To celebrate this time of year, we come together, in Spirit of good cheer
Presents a plenty and table laden, new clothes and shoes for man and maiden
Cards with warmest wishes sent, to one and all, the season's compliment To hear them dropping on the mat, heightened anticipation of "who sent that?"
At the picture first I take a glance, then read inside the sender's stance
A heartfelt message from kith and kin, a formal tone, from the less well known
Greetings warm, or formally given, driving away the day's gloom riven There's always an unexpected one, from those not heard of, or thought long gone
Good job I keep a number of cards free, to send in exchange, or calamity!
Send not a greeting in reply?! - even a mean-Spirited bod like me, would say nay A Scrooge like Spirit I do not employ, although 3 cards for the price of 1 I would enjoy!
Preparations for the great event, take many weeks and the occasional lament
A sound constitution I find helps, to ward off the bugs that Noel time helps
Fruit and nuts and a dash of honey, help stem the germs, so I can spend some money
Not too much cash needs to be spent, as a walk over the meadows brings true content
Spending a bit of dosh, on something unusual or something posh
Brings the joy of a pressy to fit the bill, hopefully, without breaking the cashier's till
It's great, the Spirit of bon amie, that Christmas brings for you and me
The Holy Spirit must be around, to inspire the prompting of such joyful sound
The laughter and joy with troubles forgotten, the love of the Lord cleansing all things rotten
To maintain this Spirit worldwide, throughout the year, would eradicate war, poverty and fear. Through the joy of sharing, by God's Mankind, the Spirit of Peace and Love, we will soon find
This aim is not a meaningless thought, to come and go as presents bought
Faith in the power of God's Love, working through Man, the Joyful Spirit of Christmas CAN
Bring Love into every heart, even where, to date, it appears to play no part
We don't all share the same view or belief in the Creator, of this we know

But maintain our Christmas Joy and Love and along the road to true happiness we will surely go

Whatever troubles around us may throng, with that Spirit of Christmas Love and Joy they won't last long

The Star of Love shining bright, will bring us safely through the darkest night

In the Spirit of God's Blessings, this Christmas we hopefully will spend

In the joy of loving company and maybe, a warming Tot or two before day's end

The Spirit of our loved ones, now in their Heavenly home, watch over us, like the shepherds, ensuring we are never alone.

19th December 2011

2012

START OF A WINTER'S DAY

Dawn seems to take an age to rise, moon still visible in the sky's Alarms have rung to help folk rise, yet no bird song heard to ease the sighs A brightening of the eastern side, springs hope that daylight soon will abide These first sightings of the dawn, precursor to the arrival of the morn

First sound of bird song on the bough, heralds the new day is now The gentle light, so slow to start, now gathers pace and uplifts the heart Distant hills as looming shapes appear, the side of Thor's Cave oh so sheer Sheep seen still sheltered under wall, protected from the night's cold squall

No snow did fall or frost gain hold, just torrential rain to wet the fold Vacuum sounds in the milking sheds, says the ladies have risen from their straw beds Daylight, under a leaden sky is through, so many sounds now commence anew Tractor with fodder for the sheep, rumbles by, it's appointment to keep

Now that we can see our way, its Bloss's premier run to start the day Down through the valley, towards the wooded glade, a sprinting hare is not afraid Up the hill he sprang into a thicket, tomorrow he could be on a sticky wicket Between man and dog a knowing look, another day he is for the cook

By the river now, it's in full flood, the caverns overflowing, no sign of mud An early swim is had today, all ice has fortunately melted away Set off once again along the trail, that once brought the steam train on a rail It picked up milk, farming stock and crops, for market and the butcher shops

Back up the lane, on to the hill today, two buzzards glide, eyeing their prey Down one swoops, it's mate looks on, a breakfasting mouse into the air is gone Atop the hill the valleys viewed, as fur and feather scavenge for food Its dull and cloudy, the winds start to raise, storm clouds from north we gaze

Aspects of this winter morn, are glorious in their shape and form In silent awe we view the cave, where in millennia past, animal and man shared the

Joe Ashton

grave Hardy cattle on the far hilltop roam, hail stones now falling, its time for home An Ash tree has fallen in the recent storm, the woodpeckers roost for many a dawn

Up the lane, homeward we go, the hail that fell now turns to snow Towels and brush awaiting on the bench, for drying and grooming after the drench Inside with a warming glow, breakfast to be enjoyed, and eaten slow The winter's day, no sound of the lark, yet still such beauty, after dark.

23rd January 2012

ODE TO THE WETTON DROUGHT

T'was the driest winter for many a year that has just passed. The parched earth of the midlands Savannah plain alas, the tumble weed blew down the dusty lane is it even drier than the plain in Spain?

I see no chance of changing fate, as sun dried skins stretch o the gate.
The buzzards on thermals upwards rise, as the heat reaches to the pale blue skys.
The cows inside, from the sun seek shade, and sheep in the meadows find a sheltered glade
Two weeks now we had to endure these climes Oil applied to ensure we continue to hear the church bell chimes.

Word spread far south about the heat, to swallows wintering in Africa Haste, haste, we must be upon the wing, summer has arrived up north, they've skipped the Spring This global warming is upon us, some learned folk do say Quick pack the grub bag and to Wetton fly, without delay.

A speedy nest we'll have to build and get some chicks made quick It won't be long before, no more grass and straw will there be to pick Will there be no point wintering in the Savannah? If Wetton is a place of continual sunshine with the warmth of Havana.

The Minister declares a hosepipe ban nationwide put a brick in the cistern and a bucket outside No this is not to catch the rain, but leaking water from the brain No washing the van or the veg, only a minute shower for the vain

Oh, wait a mow, is that a cloud above the leafless tree Yes, yes, its heading this way, will it provide some shade if only momentarily? And yet, another now I see, as black as the pudding frying for tea. Surely it won't be a moisture bearing miracle, for thee and me?

The balmy breeze that heralded this fluffy white apparition, has now turned cool
The gathering formation, now is turning dark and grey, never rain upon the way?

A bolt of thunder and lightning heralds a dramatic change, a sudden torrent into the drain
Oh yes, this is it, the climactic change, a mere tropical storm predicted by the sage.

Two weeks on from the above event, a poor camper seen floating in his tent The Wetton rains have returned home once more, 9 degrees at midday - who could ask for more!
This is more like it, winds whistling in harmony, the wet legs and wellies, for you and me too much sun and dry, a thing of the past, Wetton Spring has arrived at last

The Martins from down south, also quickly sped, relieved to find sticky wet mud to build a bed The shelter of the barn's eves an ideal construction site, no more fears of heat induced sleepless nights The usual enclosed roof and rain drain hole required, the talk of global warming long since expired The cows inside, no longer from the sun do shade, the fields too boggy for the milkmaid.

So the Drought of 2012, from Wetton long gone, the wonderful rains still pour upon The river Manifold in full flood, underground caverns no longer only mud No water butt Minister needed here, the hosepipe only used to siphon water from the beer If next month, the sight of the sun should encourage one to cast a clout A distant memory, may still hazily linger, of the 2 week Wetton Drought!!

25th April 2012

EARTH AND LIFE IN HARMONY

The silage cut and straw all baled, the sweetness of the air inhaled The Summer's growth, the crops and plants, all gathered now into their clamps Shoots of grass green, their sun kissed verdant glow, will no longer a full pasture grow Cows and sheep make the most of shortening day, before the winter feeds of silage and hay

To cope with Winter, trumpeted by loss of leaf and light, seek inner peace to fill the night
Autumn heralds dramatic change, in life of man, as in animal range
The cooling air, the loss of leaf, mimics ageing's process, the stealthy thief
The brightness of the Summer mind, dimming slightly, as thoughts and words, are sometimes hard to find

To seek and find we are told to attempt, though maybe not with such intent Seeking and striving to make the best, may not now be at our behest A time for slowing, a time for thought, time to reflect on good, not havoc wrought In the joys of these times, new thoughts arise, how to appreciate the glorious skys

No fearful thoughts of times ahead, the cold winds that will blow the icy bed
The season changes, as do I, but above the cloud, always blue sky
Sun shines at times through the gloom, to light and warm the winter room
Through the mists that pervade the hills and mind, shafts of brightness sometimes find

Roots of the grass and leafless trees, dormant appear, keep Faith and know that Spring is near Autumn and Winter will always give way, allowing Spring and Summer their time to play Each season, as with all life's phase, has special quality, to amaze Enjoy the seasons to the full, their individual aspects deserve a mull

Youth's joy of Spring and adulthood's lively Summer, may now be over
Yet, still the mellow fruits and reggae colours of Autumn's aging, fill us with mirth and strength, till Winter's ending
As with life's passage, all aspects enjoy, from transition to adulthood for both girl and boy.
The future is promised to be best of all, when our seasons are ended, and we answer God's Call.

17th September 2012

LET THE LIGHT SHINE

Through the darkness of the night, somewhere, somehow, the sun shines bright
Without our knowing, without being aware, the sun's light and warmth will be there
Through mist and rain, dark clouds and storm, the toils and troubles, all forlorn
That light above is constant and true, allow these drops of rain to strengthen, refresh, the pain in you

We know not what each cloud holds, a drop to drown, to heal the drought, or merely to wash the laden line
Of one thing we can be sure, we cannot fully understand, the plan of the One who gives us sea and land
The beauty of the rainbow the destruction of the tsunami, we sometimes think
His Creation has gone balmy
Not the balmy warmth embraced in sunlight, but the madness of a darkness filled night

To understand the wonder, contradiction and suffering of man, is something our meagre brain evades
When we add to this calamitous pot, our own mix of suffering strife and behavioural braids
To know and be sure, only a brief comfort brings, unfathomable Faith in God, is from whence Peace springs
A Peace so strong and bright, filled with the warmth, surety and comfort of Heavenly light

So where do we grasp this understanding, faith, love and insight, for which we strive?
Is it through study, living, prayer, good works and deeds, or moments of peace amongst the leaves?
Maybe there is one way to grasp the Love of the Creator One, or could it be that He allows us to create our own way?

Stepping Out Into A Good Life With Dementia

Free Will to us all He gave, to king, lord, knight and slave, so let us use this wondrous gift, to give to all life a mighty lift

The weak, the sick, the timid and oppressed with a glimpse of the Light will be greatly blessed
The Light of Love, Laughter, Joy and Praise, Support and Care, troubles and cares will help erase
Time it takes to heal pain, loss and hurt, time worth giving, to retain self worth
Let the Light of the Creator; fill us with warmth, joy and love, as our troubles he takes in exchange for His love.

Stay the course, continue the race, yes, sometimes it is tough to stay with the pace
Keep striving, in peace, with God you can be sure, you will like the rest, make it to the shore
Follow the light of His course, as best you can, knowing His Love is always mindful, you are Man
To do our best, is all he wants, with Him we forgive ourselves and others, the affronts.

So, let the Light of the Heavens, sometimes viewed as bright or dim, always guide through thick and thin
The warmth and love of the Saviour Lord, will keep us safe at home or abroad
Sometimes we are nearly lost in the things of life, all the rushing and the strife
Our lives can and will be fine, when we let the Light of the Lord's Love, through others, Shine.

13th October 2012

AUTUMN FALL

The howling winds the driving rain, late autumn trumpeted here again
Fur and fowl all shelter now, as remaining leaves strip from the bough
The strong, upright, trunk, of oak and elm exposed, the tall silver birch swaying close
A deep carpet of golden leaves below, commence to mould, before the snow

Softness of ground and the mighty stems contrast, the winter's woes they will outlast
Their bark, elephant hide, bare branch and trunk imitate, it will not matter if spring is late
As man, a few succumb to new disease, deadly spores gifted by the breeze
But even they, will be remembered for, what they were, strong and reliable, as the fir

Ditches between acres sectioned off, now flow as rivers full of froth
Brooks no longer babble, but mightily roar, the rains having provided a new score
Troughs overflow, where herds did sip, with the warmth of sun upon the hip
The hardy ewes with tups abide, not for them the shelter of beasts, that winter inside

Guns now crack, game are sprung, the dogs' job done, for their treat do long
A horn is sounded ore valley yonder, horses and hounds, after fox do wander
This strange mixture of death and life, evolving together in peace and strife
The contrasting, flow of water and siren of wind, as into winter we do descend

No, we do not descend to die, but like the mighty trunk, soar ever higher to the sky
The ones who live, the ones who die, all cared for by Creator God, even you and I!
Peace, love and life eternal, overcome the buffeting winds, that sometimes seem infernal
Life's ever shortening span, time unknown, shares autumnal joy, as we journey home.

This season of darkening days and ever extending night, may even provide respite
A chance to rest and draw breath and glimmer some meaning of life and death
In the storm, leaves stripped away, exposed are the branches that form our shape
Yes, God given beauty have we all, whether in full summer leaf, or in the autumn fall.

22nd November 2012

22nd November 2012

ADVENT THOUGHTS

"Prepare ye the way" the prophets sang, "a way for the Lord"
"What will he be like?", others asked, "will he have a chariot and sword?"
They did not know precisely nor could their imagination cope
With, how would be the Saviour Lord, His magnitude, beyond their scope

It was, in anticipation, that for centuries the faithful waited
"When He comes we will be saved", they said, "our enemies annihilated"
"The Prince of Peace" foretold they, "will first slaughter our dreaded foe"
"Then He will protect us, forever, from those who bring us woe"

So when the star, the portent one, shone brightly in the sky
The Magi Wise set off to see the Ruler from on high
The humble shepherds with their flock, an angel did awake
"Go quickly off to Bethlehem to see the King, he is no fake."

So, Shepherds and the Magi heading the same way
To Bethlehem, where the star shone brightest, that first Christmas Day
On arrival, tired and sore, in the stable they found their quest
A babe wrapped in swaddling clothes, on a straw filled manger, He did rest

These Wise men and the peasant folk, in faith, were of one mind
This infant babe truly must be, the Saviour of Mankind
And to this day, the genius and simpleton, alike, believe
A Holy Happening, is being prepared, right up to Christmas Eve

"Venio, venire", the scholars cry, "it is the verb, to come"
The apparently, not so bright, but wise, say "we are preparing for the arrival of God's Son"
Oh yes, who we await for, is the important message here
The Christ, as Man, brings Hope and Love, to share throughout each year

Once more now we prepare for the Feast, to celebrate our Saviour's birth
Yet, tis good to balance the prayerful thoughts, with joy, happiness and mirth
There is much to celebrate when Christmas Day arrives
We thank the Lord, for the good we have and woes, that with Him, we survive

Although, there are extra pressures, that upon us this season bring
Not always will we feel as though, we would like to dance and sing
But the preparations for the Feast both spiritual and lay
Are the important Advent balance, like God born Man, on Christmas Day.

2nd December 2012

ROOTS

When we are only in our youth to find our roots we need not proof. Where aged relatives came from or went, did not inspire, nor that Grandpa Murphy sang in the choir "So what", one thought, as tales of times past were regaled, of the oceans crossed, when Grandma Ashton sailed Tins of Canadian salmon, home she brought, now they were special, a young man thought Uncle Joe Murphy's name printed on the Dolymount Strand sign, did not seem anything to do with the family line. The church Uncle Willie, had built, stood fine and grand, but not as good as the adjacent beach with the golden sand. Old Grandpa Murphy offered to walk out with me one day, a polite reply from a young boy indicated "no way". To go walking out with an aged man, though your Grandpa he may be, was certainly not considered a treat by me

So into adult life we then do wend, busily constructing a path to follow, to the end As people close and little known, start to expire, thoughts start to flicker, as coals on the fire A warm glow now to fill the face, as thoughts of times and people past, do race The days at school, both good and bad the joyous days and those when sad The friends we made along the way, that helped to form us as we are today The career days, the hectic times, with life flashing by like the road marking lines Our children and their families grown, now we two can enjoy some peace alone

At the autumn stage in life, "quick start and fast" the quest for info of the past Who married who? whose child was that? where is that grave we are looking at?
The twins whose names some were sure, this certainty that was, is no more They told me this, I recall that, who was it had the three-legged cat? On it goes, the quest for information, to find out was it true that Garibaldi was a relation? We all recall we were told this and that, some coincides some does not. Small fragments of who we are and from whence we came, lead us down a windy lane

To find our roots, wherever they may be, is a daunting task for the likes of thee and me.
The hearsay, the formal records, the clues they left behind, together they form life's jigsaw, enough to blow the mind. This task now some undertake,

so a true record can be passed on, that is no fake. Remember though, we can never be sure, of all that passed in days of yore. Our own life and death, of this we can be certain, even though records of others have gone for a burton. Most important of all, is that we are children of God, He knows and loves us, not matter how odd From Him we sprung as tiny shoots, in Him we have our Faith and Roots.

5th December 2012 (Little Christmas Eve)

HOAR FROSTY MORN

The hoar frost, purina if you please, grips the bushes, now starved of all their leaves
It's crystal fingers sparkling in the foggy dawn, diamond like appearance, over lifeless thorn
Red berries, though, escape its covering gleam, the hungry birds, so grateful, on the scene
Remaining strands of feathery growth, outlined in silver threads, their skeleton shapes, still beautiful, yet dead

Magnificent, the lengthy white hedgerow, that in the spring, with blossom, overflow
Those spikey trimmed branches all neat and straight, adjacent to, the encrusted gate
The frozen ditches, that once fed the brook, now silent sheets of ice, in every nook
A sliding pheasant, sprung by the dog, may no longer stand, on yesterday's bog

The sky, so close upon the ground, the freeze fog, gently swirls around
While on the stick to ponder and absorb this wondrous sight, a special moment captured, is always right
Absorb this majestic view within, a beauteous scape so rare, culminating with the bound of the winter coated hare
Warmer air, will no doubt soon, ease this frost away, though pictureous memory of its visit, will forever stay.

12th December 2012

CHRISTMAS JOY

However long or short our lives are, each and every one, travels afar
We may never leave, the home of our birth, but still we travel life's journey forth
From babe to child, then youth to man, a remarkable journey, this lifespan
Times of learning, never ending, tasks and duties ever descending

Stick at it with vigour, hope and joy, just like the Christ man, from a boy
Even He, at times, though of God above, did, in His humanity, need love
Mary and Joseph, in the stable cared, with Wise men and shepherds who stood and stared
Confusion and awe both fused in one, puzzled at the sight of God's own Son

What does this mean when Angles sing? "News of a Saviour Son, to you we bring"
A Saviour who we never see, not like the folks in Galilee
We see Him, not now upon the earth, yet He is with us, e'en before our birth
Watching over every step we take, through every triumph and mistake

Every stage of life through which we move, He watches, guides us, through rough and smooth
We cannot be alone you see, even at times, it seems like, there is only you or me
The Christ Child, now Godhead and Man, has come to help and always can
Each day, whether having more pain than joy, can be given over to the infant boy

He knows the path our lives do travel and every crisis, will help unravel
Every joy with us He shares, as with each opportunity, to show He cares
Although we slip and sometimes fall, His love for us, overcomes all
Thank You God, for sending Your Son, to bring the chance of Peace and Joy for everyone

He shares with us our joy and woe and never leaves us, wherever we go
Along the winding path of life, He stays aside us, girl, boy, woman, man, husband and wife

Joe Ashton

An example He gave, with lowly birth, those Kings and shepherds sharing, wonder and mirth
For believers and sceptics, His true love will endure; we are all children of God, both rich and poor

As the star shone over that stable of birth, a new Son came for all the earth
The Saviour Jesus, as He became known, is still with us today and will welcome us home.
So this Christmas be merry and playful and fun, remembering Christ came for everyone
From cradle to grave and stable to cross His Love never dwindles and is never lost.

22nd December 2012

YEAR OLD and NEW are NIGH

The year we have, fast fades into the past, though another one approaches very fast
Assemble thoughts of things gone by and also those, our way, are nigh
Looking forad and aft, to port and starboard, knowing not what is ahead
Understanding the happenings of the past, may cause one toss abed

Fun and joy, tears and sighs, every year does bring, as well as times of mighty laughter following
We celebrate the birth and mourn the death, with equal spirit given
Welcoming in new life on earth and rejoice, the passing into Heaven
The glory of creation, the coming and the growing, both share, the fading of our knowing

Triumphs and tragedies, not always in equal share, in the midst of all, know, God is there
To join in the fun and laughter the sadness and the tears
These we know are part and parcel of all our years
Anticipation of the Good ahead, were all in this together, whether trial or joy is fed, nothing lasts forever

Opportunities the new year always brings, chances of advancement, in many, many, things
Moving ever onward in relationship and life. The ever-growing love of friends, partner or wife
Understanding what happens, as we stride or crawl each day, is not necessary, to find our way
Forth in faith and joy, if you do or don't, believe, will be the lifesaver in the pack, this New Year's Eve

Making resolutions, a very laudable game, even though I break them all each year, just the same
Doesn't stop them being considered, these noble aspirations, if only a wish of peace and love among all nations

Joe Ashton

Go easy on yourself; don't be beating oneself up, maybe share a something with others, from the loving cup
Rejoice now for the passing year and whatever the new may bring, Hosanna, to the Lord above for everything.

29th December 2012

2013

MID WINTER MUSE

A time of year, a phase of life, some dread or treat with disdain
A time to moan, a time to groan, fed up with snow and rain
Yet, is there nothing good, this mid-season time can bring?
Oh yes there is, I hear some say, snowdrops heralding future Spring

The wind is howling, rain lashes the meadows snow
The thaw set in, ice water no place to go
Brooks, gulleys, drains and troughs full to overflow
Thick ice lying on hill bottom, no escape for it's melting oh!

Everywhere so stark and silent, just as before the dawn
Only far off cry, of bird of prey, or was it a hunting horn?
No movement of fur or fowl, oh how we hunter's morn
Wait! is that a rustle in the bank, a slightly moving thorn?

Examining dead hedge rows, a close peering gives a clue
Hey! They're not entirely dead, those elder, beech and yew
Leaves stripped yes and branches bare, a real deathly hew
But closer inspection of the branch at last provides a clue

A tiny budlet, all neatly formed, is there for all to see
Is this the sign of coming life, that awaits for you and me?
A time of warmth, love and colour, awaiting us to be
As the snow drop, we will survive, life's barren entity

Enjoy each time, that we are gifted, give yourself a shove
The cold, storm and healing thaw, support of those we love
The darkness and cold season's strife will pass as clouds above
Mid-winter season moves along, all part of Creator's love

Though some gloom, this time provides, we never need despair
It won't be long till buds are open and lambs dance everywhere

Joe Ashton

Suckling pigs already born, calves in the sheds are fair
Out into the meadows they will go and visitors returning upon the air

An amazing aspect then, does this mid-season bring,
Appearing dead, though much alive, in all and everything
On the day of our departing, pray, don't let us want to cling
Rejoice and Praise God's Love for Us, while entering His new Spring.

28th January 2013

MISTS OF TIME

The minutes come, the hours go, this is the time that we all know
This gift of time our life does fill, with healthy joy, or sometime of ill
What to do to fill this time, the gift to us, both yours and mine
To activate, a busy schedule or cunning plan, or just to say; "relax Man"

Those choices, they present each day, as morning mists do drift away
The busy schedule, formerly held, no longer drives this life, so meld
More focus now on depth and joy, as it was when just a boy
The time came with mist and snow and so many places where to go

On scooter now, up to the rec, to play at footie, what the heck
Forget the homework; they gave us none, time for playing in the sun
Folks back then seemed very big, enormous hat, maybe it hid a wig?
Baggie clothes and floral patterns set the scene, until the coming of the jean

These visions of things past, seem so very clear, not blurred by today's fog I fear
Some days it comes, some days it goes, sometimes it's not there, who knows?
It does not matter whether clarity or shade, enjoy the garden with the spade
Clear the mist from out the head yourself, so what if you can spy an elf!

The mist of mind we all endure, either later on, if not before
Comes and goes, as does the time, this mist it is both yours and mine
Having a joyful element too, it shades the harshness that once we knew
It softens edges and blurs the line, oh yes there's joy, in Mists of Time.

26th February 2013

SUCCESS and FAILURE

We strive to succeed, to be the best, to finish ahead of all the rest
To triumph and to come in first, to hear the loud applause, outburst
On top, premier, first past the post, it is the winning we like most
The summit to be reached we strive, as worker bees, back to the hive
Constantly seeking the ultimate goal, that's ok, but don't forget the Soul

Less than perfect is how we are born, all helpless, exposed and forlorn
Protection then we greatly need, depending on others to succeed
If, as babes, we are to survive, we need the love and toil as others strive
That team work, full of loving heart, ensures our safe arrival at the start
Now we have safely come to earth, this was no accident, our birth

Not of our making, this miracle of life, a Creator's gift to man and wife
To understand this phenomenon, only God truly knows what is to come
A safe arrival, life lived to the full, a happy death, that won't be dull
Contribution we do make, but triumphant outcome, we do not always take
Sometimes we fail to succeed, maybe this is good and what we need?

Success and failure, strange bed fellows they, a cause of joy and dismay
Yet what is triumph and fulfilment of plan, when failure may lead to a better man?
This betterment, of a living being, caused by a failure to those who've seen
How can this be, we ponder now, the dismantling of some sacred cow
To fail, can lead to triumph of another kind, both indeed and mind

Failure and success, go hand in hand, to develop balance throughout the land
Successful, sometimes fail and losers sometimes win, the divide between the two is oh so thin
A successful failure at His behest, from depths of lowliness came the best
That infant king in manger, worshiped, lay, who on the cross would have His day
Triumph and failure His life and death appeared to say, until he rose on Easter Day.

10th March 2013

HAPPY ST PATRICK'S DAY

To those of us with Irish Blood, growing inspiration from out the mud
A little green flower, a massive message did portray
Tis why we celebrate St Patrick's Day
The brigands and the warring tribes, laid down their arms, when St Pat arrived
A simple message, on a complicated theme, a 3 in one, they had never seen
Peace and Love was his main prayer for the wild folk in County Clare
Throughout the land, his message spread, as up Croagh Patrick, he did tread
Atop the summit he did stay, a while to eat and a while to pray
His job done, War Lords at peace, the snakes all scarpered from the heath
So now we celebrate St Pat's great gift, with a pint of the hard stuff to give a lift
Of this we know he would approve, though a Saintly Man, he was never a prude
Celebrate with prayer, laughter and joy, wearing that shamrock plant he did employ
A massive message, Patrick told, as relevant today, as in times of old
We thank you Lord for the gift of Pat, the roots he gave us and the craic
A Celtic nation can be proud to shout his name out very loud
So thank you St Pat, for visiting Ireland's shore, bringing peace and love, to be sure
When we are long gone, they will still say, have a great St Patrick's Day.

15th March 2013

SPRING ARRIVES

The sun is shining, 14-degree heat, 16th April oh so neat
Balmy, south westerly, blows all day, final bones of winter melt away
Daffodils start swelling yellow; "burst open now, there's a good fellow"
Tiny blue bells have come forth, between tree, shelter from cold north
Ancient church, it's bells peeling, raised eyes to heaven's azure ceiling
The warmth of the sun, an inner glow; "tis the spring alright, you know"
Birds of varying shape and size, at frantic nest building all do strive
Putting behind them dark winter's day, to get procreating without delay
Nature is shooting forth, at frenetic pace, time to catch up in the race
To start creation cycle once again, so plant, bird and animal can remain
Long, long, winter, delayed everything, including the very start of spring
But now, it's here, it's grip is firm, starting anew, for us all to learn
Though wintry life be cold and dark, twill give way to the song of lark
A curlew sounds it's meadow call; "we are back to roost until the fall"
Blackbird sings a glorious trill, as evening sun, sky reddens still
A morning chorus, new flowers a day, toads a mating, hip hip hurray
Now we know, in spite of delay, the joy of spring arrived today.

16th April 2013

LIFE'S SEASONS

The embryonic features of life within the womb are simulated in the Spring, as seeds begin to germ.
The buds swell upon the branch; the blossoms start to form, just as animal and plant, get ready to be born.
The warming moisture swells the growth, the forms take shape of life, the buck and doe prepare the nest, as do husband and wife.
Soon the due day dawns, the blossom bursting forth, the new-born babes of mice and men arrive in various forms.
Must survive those early days, winds a blow, sometimes rain and forceps at the birth. T 'is what the babes of manimal and plants endure, soon followed by great mirth.

Summer's warming sun hastens joyful growth of day. With shortening night and mouths to feed, Fantastic Monsieur Reynaud, seeks his prey.
The meadows full of playful sounds of beast, fur and wing. The children playing in the park, while mothers to growing babes, sing.
Eventually the heat subsides, and calmness fills the air, the young of Spring have now grown up, as Autumn's mists we share.
Beauty of colours on the bough, before leaves fall to ground, the glory of creation viewed, with lessening of sound.

God's natural world conjoined with human, as we go. Interdependent, in awe of each, before the winter's snow.
To use this time wisely, we do try, adjusting to how things are. Squirrel collects the nuts and migratory flee afar, while some people boil up fruit and store it in a jar.
The babes, beasts and wildlife, all, now fully grown, prepare for the shortening days and lengthening nights, while some retire alone.
The arrival of the winter, mixed blessings it may bring. A chance to trust in God made Man and His praises to sing.
We may be grey like hoare frost, tho just as beautiful, inside. The innocence of children, awaiting Santa on his ride.

Others have grown old now, not knowing what is in God's plan, till it does unfold for each, a differing lifespan.

Joe Ashton

The turkey and the goose, the pig and too the cow, the vegetables grown throughout the year, all have great significance now.
So, we, like they, when life's winter has its fling, still have much joy and mirth and love, along with us to bring.

We may now do it in a different way, not as in days of yore. None the less, what we think and say, surely, is as relevant as before?
This ending season also brings great beauty, as well as joy and mirth and even more time for snoozing and a loosening of the girth.
The hibernators keeping warm and snug, with plenty of fat on board, Brock Badger,
Squirrel Nutkin and the Pensioner, if fuel he can afford.
The Seasons, Man, Animal, Plant and all Creation, inter dependent and entwined, may be a glimpse of God's love for us and what He has in mind.
To serve each other, as best we can, appreciating the beauty and joy, each season brings, provides an opportunity to honour and appreciate the Creator of all things.

26th June 2013

SILENCE

Silence, in peace, outward and in, sheds light for the soul, where to begin
Inner depth, our inmost strength, whence we search, sometimes at length
Silent thought, through noise and clamour, no depth can reach or enamour
A quiet time, an open space, will shelter from the challenging race

No escape, ex joys or woes, but a chance to share with ONE who knows
Silent thoughts, creating deafening sound, good to take to higher ground
A moment's pause, in life's surf alone, then safe to shore, on gentle foam
One's inner depth, need hold no fear, dark chasm deep, will soon be clear

Created by ONE, who sent His Son, there's quiet peace for everyone
In silence, listening to the Word, can free heart and mind of all absurd
The peace and joy, silence can bring, lifts heart and soul upon the wing
Soaring high o'er troubled earth, leaving space for perspective, joy and mirth

A happy, healthy, vision to gain, when silence given chance to reign
A quiet moment, inter noisy hour, as glimpse of sun, between the shower
Silent refreshment, for both soul and Being, clearer insight on everything
In silence, oft the loudest message gained, of love, joy and peace, obtained.

13th September 2013

CHRISTMAS APPROACHES

Just as in times, long ago, when the thought of Christmas brought a glow
Anticipation, joyous sounds, fun and laughter, throughout, abounds
Decorations dusted down, tree lights checked, before going to town
The tree this year, will it be a real or artificial? Either will do, that's official!

Cards to write, some with ease, others need special message, to please
Have you got their address, holly or snow, for those folks we knew, long ago?
Where was it they lived before? Have they now gone to another shore?
Will soon find out if their still around or are now nestling in hallowed ground!

Present hunting, along with the crowd, boisterously joyful, even very loud
Sally Army band, playing tunes old and new, we stand around to get a view
The coloured lights now shining bright light up the marketplace at night
The Mods and Rockers hung out here, now long gone, as yesteryear

A crib, depicting the Christmas scene, alongside the ice rinks winter theme
Shrieks of laughter, fun and joy, all praise and thanks be to that Holy Boy
He brought the message of Hope for all, the young and old, big and small
Keep the balance, if you can, remember, he was the Son of God made Man

The time is flying, can't wait too long, much and all as we enjoyed the song
Paper wrapping, bows and string, at Christmas we seem to need everything
Midst the chaos, bustle, stress and strain, rely on Him who came to reign
For us all He came, from above, to receive and share His Christmas Love.

11th December 2013

<u>2014</u>

LIFE'S MYSTERY

From whence we came, where forth we go, Mystery, even now
The science of it all, the humble prayer, do not answer everything out there
Explore the mind, the heart, the soul, too seek an answer may be the goal
Bright or dim, we take a similar path, unexplained, the Mysteries amass!
To strive for understanding, noble thing, if this knowledge, peace does bring
Peace of heart and mind combined, a glorious outcome for all to find

What of our troubles then, that interrupt the peace, stillness and joy?
We know we cant avoid such times, no easy solution, for girl or boy
To understand, this quirk of fate or cunning plan, is it of God or Man?
Do we need to know at all, will knowledge ease the pain, maybe it can?
The Mystery path, could be another way, to knowing without understanding
Struggling, asking why and how, may, for some, result in a happy landing

Peace, joy, trouble and strife, constitute for all, the Mystery of life
A bit of all, to life's table we bring, to digest all together, is the thing
An mix of these, we experience and employ, eclectic our sadness and joy
The Mysterious ability and strength unseen will, in time, rebuild our being
Sometimes forlorn our efforts fine, carry on, twill be no waste of time
Some stage, not known to science or Man, Mystery will ensure you can.

12th January 2014

I DON'T LIKE MONDAYS

"I DONT LIKE MONDAYS" a former Blackrock lad did sing
A sentiment, many will agree, as they awake for first cup of coffee
Oh yes, one, children also share, as tangles are roughly pulled from hair
Started working week on Monday morn, excited expectation, rarely the norm

So maybe you, empathise with the sentiments of this, less than witty ditty
If so, take heart, there is a brighter horizon to which you sail, both fe and male
"Retirement", may seem a far-off dream, when alarm, each Monday, does ring
Toil and early rising, rich reward will bring, sunny walk listening to birds sing

"Smug thoughts these", adding to your woe, I hear you workers say
WELL NO, take heart, best is yet to come, yes, Monday peaceful, in the sun
Monday, could it ever be, the best weekday, I hear you say?
The answer is YES, take it from me, as I sit relaxing with cup of tea.

Pressured times, now long gone, so can listen to bird song in the sun
"Monday", they sing, "its here again", so let's rejoice, with that refrain
Mondays now I like the best, relax, have fun, no strife
Able now to, peacefully say, thank you God for MONDAY.

Monday 20th January 2014

THAT CELTIC HERO

Did he, hurling, rugby, or GAA play? Maybe he did, in his own way
Was this the sporting trio he did preach? a way to the Trinity, within reach
Shamrock he used, a flower so green, to help us know a God unseen

Snatched from his homeland, with sail and oar, sailing far to Erin's shore
First a slave, the least of the flock, one who many would only mock
Then inspired, in later youth, with fearsome courage, he preached the truth

High King listened with intent, seeing now what Patrick's shamrock meant
Free at last to spread the Word, about the God of whom no one had heard
A mighty message did he bring, via tiny plant from Ireland's spring

Pat's message travelled throughout the land - Bog of Allen to Silver strand
Word, no border could withstand, all conquering truth in St Patrick's Ireland
And so today let's celebrate St Pat's life and love that makes Ireland great.

16th March 2014

THE EASTER FEAST

That special time again is here; let's celebrate Easter with love and cheer
A festival of Faith the season Spring - joy, fun, love and prayer, do bring
Egg broken open, as the tomb, taste buds arising before noon
New lambs frolic in the field, the promised life to come will yield
Time to enjoy the Light hurray, the darkened days now gone away

A sacrifice, by the Son made Man, a cross borne in hope, so that we can
In faith and trust at Eastertide, those lingering doubts, firmly cast aside
Enjoy the gifts we've been endowed and of those we have not, rejoice aloud
For we are not expected to do just everything, even though it is the Spring
Thank God, for what we have and do, a winning team, Him, me and you

The risen, Easter Lord, for us has paved, a life eternal, beyond the grave
Now is the time, take heart and sing, a joyful Eastertide will bring
New hope and strength, we can find, for those whose life has been unkind
A prayer that, new strength they will obtain, to ease body and mind of pain
Joy, Peace and Hope be ours today, as the Easter Feast gets under-way.

17th April 2014

PRAY SILENCE!

A silent prayer, it needs no words, to an all loving, all seeing, all knowing, all mighty,
God. Acknowledgement that He exists and loves us is enough, without burdensome, prayerful litany. He's taken all our woes on board, none of our issues ever ignored.
Concerns complex, of humankind, lovingly carried, relieved the mind.
Unburdened, free to fly like birds upon the air, to heights unfathomed as deep and yet up there. Whether up or down we wish to soar, He, with us always, when rich and poor.
Our freedom given, of Will, from birth, to be sad or glad, with triumph and mirth.
To fight the fight, that daily struggle brings, sticking in Faith, borne up on those wings.
Those storm clouds that, come menacingly near, will be blown away, have no fear!
The warming sun, the refreshing breeze, return to harmonise the rustling leaves.
Their joyful song, this summer day, lift spirits heavenward, as we easily pray.
With sun drenched light, sky azure blue, surely all is well for me and you?
Yes, it is, Thank God, we cry, all is well for you and I. Yet, this is not the case for everyone, some with yokes still heavy and burdensome. So for them Lord, a deafening cry, not silent prayer this day. Pray, lift their burdens, give them hope that they too may fly and too rejoice in the freedom of the sky.

6th July 2014

WHO DOES NOT PRAY?

Prayers are things we say and do, simple things, bit like me and you!
Simple, complex, laissez faire, all are elements of people's prayer
A life of prayer is led by all, whether in the church or at the Ball

We all pray, many times a day, in smiling greetings or enjoying play
The kind word, the authentic reprimand, are all prayers, you understand
Amazed, some maybe, to find they pray, as you and me

"I do not pray" say you to I; "oh so what about the coin you gave that guy?"
The act of kindness, or gift to one in need, is nothing, if not prayer indeed
As too, a brief thought for God or Man, in appreciation of what we can

What we can't, does not matter a jot, not when viewing another's lot
A thankful moment, let it be, for what the Lords' given you and me
To enjoy fun and laughter, and sorrows share, all of this is real prayer

Creation, all around we see, whether city dwelling or by the sea
Admiring the beauty that surrounds, mixed with clamorous sound
Use of our senses in every way, appreciating all, is how we pray

If one thinks; "I never pray", no, tis only prayer recognition, in delay
Formal, informal, in every way, just living our lives, each and every day
We consciously or inadvertently say, many a prayer, in our own way.

22nd July 2014

CHANGE

The seasons come and go, just as the tide does ebb and flow, at behest of the moon
Waters recede, golden sands leave, walked upon for only hours, as they return so soon
While time is now, the most to make, striving on, wide awake, no floating like balloon
Preparing for the times ahead, though around the corner, maybe instead, the unexpected loom
Mixture may, of anticipated day, or night ahead planned, surprise us with both bright and gloom

What are we to do with altering times, the joy and lament they bring, stay firm and steadfast how?
Draw on the past, maybe only yesterday, a time when all went well, twill ease the need for furrowed brow
Each moment of time, present or a gone by age, have treasure in their store, to enlighten what is now
Experience gained, from failure or success, a light it shines the way, onward, forward, with shoulder to the plough
Task that seemed so difficult, completed and peace re-gained, time to ponder and enjoy the inner calmed thou

What is today? maybe tomorrow gone, or possibly still there plus more, refreshing mix of old with new
A seasonal time, that went so well last year, we try to recreate with more cheer, some bits old, plus a few
The beauty of the golden leaf, the pheasant mature and grand, these gifts of nature, God, help us think of You
An inexplicable joy, comfort of recognisable change, alteration that is meant to be, the One we know is true
"Go with the flow" we say to you; "relax just swim along", though for some this is with ease, for not all, will it do

Opportunities come our way, some we just let go, others never come to stay and for that we can be glad

Joe Ashton

We were not meant to have them on board, why we do not know, without them now, there is no need to be sad
That leaf filled branch no nest did hold, the brook without a fry, mystery of choices made, with many options had
Some things we alter as we go, sometimes to repeat and others no, for the opportunity to choose, you bet I'm glad
Times and people, fashions and fads, constantly come and go, life evolves and alters each day, 'twill be our life we had.

7th October 2014

WAR

What is war, but a politician's plaything, a destructive, song to sing
Under the shade of a righteous banner, better than the sickle and hammer?

Protect and shield we must invade, down the enemy whoever they may be
Was it not a perceived terrorist at Calvary, that Pilate crucified on a tree?

Weak leadership must not be present, demonstrate strength to the peasant!
Leaders weakness, seals our fate, bunkered in safety, as others lay prostrate

Clinging to power, under the guise of justice and mercy, is their lowest hour
Millions are spared the lie, off to war away from daughter, son and wife, to die

In search of power, and historical honour, good folk sent as cannon fodder
To what end the tragic slaughter leads? Only to more unfulfilled, political needs

Thirst for power and glory unquenched, "invade" cry the "Front Bench"
A righteous case soon put together, in Dispatch Boxes of finest leather

From the neutered Ministerial Aide, a moralistic ethical case to Invade
Forget outcome, suffering and plight, that's on a far offshore, ok to ignore!

Honour, valour, are the cry as ignorant politicians send them off to die
Time, immemorial, goes on this waste of life, for vane inglorious strife

Every nation bears the scar, from political leaders who went too far
Their remit serve the nations, strong, weak and poor, NOT MAKE WAR!

9th November 2014 (Remembrance Sunday)

LITTLE WORLD

Join me in my little world, a while, a place of joy and fun
Though sometimes, like everyone else, an occasional rumbling tum
A fantasy, a reality, each has their place within
The cold hard fact melted into warmth, the rubbish in the bin

To see the sky all blue and black, a beauty both they are
The sun, the snow, the wind, the storm, through them we all walk far
The music of the traffic or even of the birds
The cymbalic clash of cherub wings, hovering, never heard

Though small this world of imagery, yet massive nonetheless
A contradiction in so many ways, of concentration divest
Not always needing to be, upon the ball today
Many a time tis better, to let the memories play

Of fun and cheer, of sadness gone, a heady mix for sure
All co-equal in this little world, mixed up with sow and boar
Appreciating all around, though not in every way
Happy for them to visit, though not this very day

A small, yet very real world, I inhabit, just like you
A differing meaning for us all, whether seen as black or blue
Those creatures may be friends to me or maybe food to you
However, tis we view them all, a moments cud we chew

The clanking tram, the hooting owl, commuters spewing fumes
All have little worlds to traverse, morning and afternoons
A heady mix of folk and life, all moving at a pace
Step off a while, if you can and join the "Human" race

The sun is setting now, upon my little world today
Thank you, God, for letting me view it in this way
The orange glow through window streams, last light of day afore night
This is one life I love, the only one I have, till tomorrow bright.

23rd November 2014

TAKING OURSELVES TOO SERIOUSLY?

Such are the pressures of the day, many of our own making, hey?
"Bring them on" we seem to say, to all pressures; "come our way"
Why look for more trouble in our life, why not turn away from strife?
Do we have to be in the thick of it, joining the bear fight in the pit?
Pause a while, this very day, - think;" does it have to be this way?"

Every problem, do we have to solve? Why not let someone else take hold?
Allowing others space and time, to resolve their issues, is this just fine?
Do they not also have the gift, to give themselves and others a lift?
Of course they do, good to see, no need to, just rely on you and me?
Awake today, to that new dawn;" was it to save the World I was born?"

No, there came a Babe one year, who brought the answer to relieving fear
Relax, enjoy, have fun, with the Love, of that infant Child from above
He shows the way, relieves the pain, leads us on through loss and gain
Its not all us, upon our own, those joys and sorrows, he too does own
Carrying us along each day, so, "Don't take ourselves too seriously" I say!

13th December 2014

2015

THOUGHTS

Are they just imaginary moments lost on the winds of time?
Are they inspired by a subconscious movement, oh so fine?
Good or bad, they come our way, in multiples, throughout the day.
When sleeping they are real, unseen, just given the nominee of dream.

The mind alive, with thought does thrive, on cunning plot or itching hive
The meandering moment, saved or lost, arrives and departs, without cost
Too complex to grasp, a depth of meaning, another comes, off the ceiling
No action required, by these interlopers, just enjoy, so called no hopers!

Understanding of what they deliver, brief and momentary, not a long liver
They come and go every moment, a sumptuous feast of each exponent
Music and mayhem, they can bring, maybe better for recipient to sing
Received now, the new idea once held its old, lost with others in mould.

Chink of light, flash of brilliance, keep them coming they help resilience
Every new moment that they bring, can be the start of one's new Spring
Keep open the track from whence they come, never stop what has begun
Seemingly mad, or seemingly daft, a Good Thought is the best we have.

13th January 2015

RISK TAKER'S PRAYER

Grant me Lord the faith to say, guide the risks I take today
Sureness of safety and peace achieved, still requires risk indeed
Challenging the accepted way, leaves open to chance, others say; "nay"
Opening the mind, bold actions they, always a risk in what we do each day

Surmount barriers, the security of fear, remain unlocked, inner joy here
A step unknown, whether forward or back, all is well with Faith in the pack
Trust in the guiding hand, unseen, though always there
Unseen and strong, on which to rely, however undertakings fare

A strange new place and folk to meet, or just an unfamiliar street
This way or that, to follow, dodging through streets, like Swift or Swallow
Decision now, we have to take, leaving all fear in our wake
Move on, try this way to go, be not afraid to make mistake

From errors learnt, our future made, take courage, firm foundations laid
Another gain, through risk today, may in the long run, greatly pay
Advance and discovery achieved; courage combined with faith indeed
Lord, help me each day, risk faith in you, to succeed.

28th January 2015

OUR PEARL

Facing the truth is all fine and well, but do not let it become, a living hell
Accept the challenge it may bring, after winter comes the spring
Potential ensnarement lurking there, avoid it now, with joy and care
See through confusion, to beyond, listen to the music, a joyous sound

Slowness of thought, deeper fathoms reach, no need for constant speech
A quiet, yet active, thought process this, untangling dross and clearing mist
Cutting through spume, bow surge it makes, swirling eddies in its wake
Land from the water, a different perspective, a different view and so effective

New challenge today, whatever may be, deal with it calmly, over tea
Every new puzzle a solution holds, keep the faith, while truth unfolds
No heroic abandon, to drug induced alarm, just a moment of quiet and calm
Can't find answers, when none to give, just enjoy the life we live

Adapting to change, a must life long, follow the music and join in the song
Sound may not correspond to music notation,
Doesn't matter in this oration "Courage", is all we need to sing,
if you fear duff notes, then earplugs bring
No callous disregard for sensitivities this, just plain speaking, a Hit or Miss

Thoughts moving, with the tide of day, sometimes full in, then ebbing away
Draw of the moon, the mists can't hide, there is always movement inside
What can't be seen is still there, even when reliant on others to care
Our shell may be battered from the tide, yet still our Pearl rests inside.

12th February 2015

SHORT THOUGHT

Short thoughts, though, as small they be, provide, as lift, atop the highest tree
Instant, springs their inspiration, sometimes a view, beyond distant nation
Tired and sleepy following the way, hear Vespers chant, at end of day
A thanksgiving, for all that has been, the love of life and those unseen

Away and far, though some may be, not to be viewed from this tree
A thought, like prayer, a praise, an ask, to help cope with every task
Thanks for all we have and those we love, those daily blessings from above
Take the rest the evening brings; recharge batteries, for even finer things

Onward, forward, round the bend, make joyful the journey, till the end
Lighten hearts with fun, not forgetting the One, who created moon and sun
A gift He gave, whose paths we crossed, watching, seeing, we don't get lost
Together, a way forward sought, looking for the sign, from one short thought.

24th February 2015

THE MOMENT

It fleeting comes and then off goes, as spring blossom or melting snows
The here is now, soon to be past, future time, not here to last
This is the moment, the very now; make the most of it, somehow
Coming fast and then away, those opportunities of every day

Time never waits for you, they say, the inward tide slips fast away
Though it returns later that day, the sands themselves, have moved away
The currents live and moving fast, nothing static ever lasts
Living, growth, movement made, even when lazing in the shade
Mind and heart, active still, slumber closed eyes, disguise the Will
Carry on, fill the day, take opportunities, before they go away
Keep it real, yet hit the high, always reaching for the sky
Slowing maybe, some things forgot, making every MOMENT mean a lot.

21st March 2015

EASTER THOUGHTS

Sun rises earlier each morn, than winter, when it failed to warm
Birdsong pervades, though branches still bare, sign of bud opening there
Woodpecker heard, hammering for a lark, waking grubs inside the bark
Tis time of year to arise, as feathered visitors, fill the skys

Feast of conquering death forever, the trials of life, even dodgy weather
Jumping lambs in pastures new, is what life has to offer ewe
Newborn, like blossom, breaking forth, cracking egg, announcing birth
A shriek of pain, a cry of joy, from death to life for girl and boy

Celebrating the Risen, in spirit and mind, even joy for those, still left behind
Faith and Hope it's said; "springs eternal", just as nut forms from the kernel
Visions of lively things anew, pictured in mind, though not in full view
Positivity, the gift of today, granted by the One, who in a tomb lay

So now to celebrate a Lenten end, small sacrifice, trying not to offend!
To mix these times of God and Man, is surely, the best We can
We, of Him, come into life, with help of His joy, cope with strife
He, to thank this Easter time, the God made Man, risen to shine.

1st April 2015

CYCLE OF LIFE

BANG, start of the great swim for Life, all caused by God, man and wife
The race is on for that Golden prize, a chance to develop brain and eyes
Competitors on either side swimming strong, tails swishing wide
Avoiding now opponents wash, as waves and current make a splash
Before, maybe only, seconds long, we are First home, from all the throng.

Golden egg, a home awhile, refuge from the storm, warming place to form
Nine months of relaxing swims, in calm waters, forming brain and limbs
Food a plenty, of varying kind, developing digits, eyes and mind
Genetic formation occurring too, many other things making Me and You
Then to complete the job a whole, the good Lord, also, provides a Soul

One morn awake, Ooops! We're off, like water rushing from the trough
The warming fluid starts to ebb away and wall open and closes as we pray;
"Yike's! another adventurous journey maybe, just have to wait and see"
Suddenly, a massive shove, then out we pop in headlong rush
Where are we now, we start to blink, whack on the bottom makes us think!

Arriving in a new world to find, strange shapes and sounds invade the mind
Go with the flow the only way, they love and care for us, so that's ok
Recognition comes a pace, always enjoying a familiar face
The Ooos and coos they sound amuses us, as does journeying on the bus
Knowing some, by scent and sound of name, Mum and Dad always remain

Babe to infant, then young girl or boy, a forming time to enjoy
Dependent still on loved one's care, though growing independence there
Child to Manhood rapidly fills, prepared, in part, to climb life's hills
Fully independent, then left home, loving, working caring for one's own
Offspring's children very Grand, oft scattered across the land

Life's autumn time sets in, no longer the draw and excitement, of life's din
Time to enjoy a slower pace; just take part in Seniors race
Younger, now help, support and care, though different, we are still there
The waters now in which we bathe we hope to enjoy until the grave
Relaxing in the life anew just developed further, Me and You.

15th April 2015

NOT TO DESPAIR

Sometimes the things, no longer, or, never there, create within, a major care
Where and why have they gone, or why did I have none?
Where is the hope I never had, that turns all good from bad?
Has it gone, was it in the air, the faith that carried me on, from here to there?

This care, created by times of doubt, as soon as can, to be; "kicked out"!
To doubt, to fear, attributes of human nature are, just to be stopped, from going too far
Every skill and tactic employ, many learnt as a growing girl or boy
Raising one's spirit to a higher level, we can, with the help of God and Man

Solid tree trunk, branches gently heave, still there, though now covered by leaves
Times of concern, unrealistic goals to achieve, these oft cover us like the leaves
Remember this, at times of strife or woe; your solid trunk continues to grow
Your inner core, your being, unknown to most, carried by a heavenly host

You may not believe in the greater Being, that endless love, sometimes unseen
Forsake not, nor give up on hope and joy, they will return, if right tactic we employ
What is this magic, cunning plan, to bring back happiness and peace to Man?
I do not know, cannot say, all I believe is, twill happen one day, this gift for ALL, I pray.

14th May 2015

STRIVING

Each day dawns, a new challenge to meet, including, new folk to greet
They carry their pack too, mix of goodies for and from, me and you
Coming and going, in thought and mind, all trying best, striving to be kind
Don't try too hard, just enough, to keep the world from taking the huff

Folk chasing a new goal, onward yet, Striving for body and soul
Creating steam and pressure each day, is this a progressive way?
Deal with issues, in calmness, worth a try, leave worries to our God guy
Strive to relieve the pressure of the day, with a little fun and joy, in some way

Challenges, yes, take them on board, along with help of the Almighty Lord
Problems solved, many times each day alive, carrying us forward as we Strive
Does not have to be all stress and strife, let music, fun, joy and love, fill life
Love of life, a worthy Strive, helps daily purpose, be more than just survive

Now, thank God, we are not all be the same, some like sun and others rain
Each one created a special way, still Striving all, to get through each day
Everyone with a different plan, how to balance in mind, both God and Man
Insights different, for each alive, lets not too greatly Strive, just let Spirit guide.

31st May 2015

BIRTHDAY EVE

Years come, then they go, onward we venture, each and every day
The hills we climb, in valleys taken refresh, finding odd times to pray
Not in desperation, but in ease, a chat with the Lord above
Whose constant care and guiding hand lifts us all, in love

Sometimes we miss the obvious, the plain to see and more
The living, breathing, Spirit, moving in our midst, guides, inside and outdoor
Blessed with time to enjoy reflection, among the moving blades
The grasses and trees and hedgerows deep, provide the cooling shade

A time for gratitude to one and all, who help along the way?
Not always easy for them now, not knowing what one may say
Nevertheless, as loving and faithful, as the day that we first met
The Special one, became my wife, whose love never failing, I experience yet

A lucky chap, that is myself, fortunate in so many ways
No, not luck, just many blessings I have received, upon all these days
Family and friends, so far and near, not to stay too long
A brief encounter, now and again, to share the sweet bird song

One does not need great time, or space, to share in what is good
Another year has passed with speed to man, sharing equally, boyhood
Memories of the younger days, now so evidently crystal clear
Time to celebrate, blessings and love experienced, as in yesteryear

8th June 2015

FATHER'S DAY MUSE

They come in various shapes and size, multi cultural, daft, stupid and wise
Most link these attributes in one, lucky to be blessed with daughter and son
An accidental fate or Divine plan, for sure fatherhood is not in the gift of man
An honour and gift, not won or earned, nor even through earnest study learned
Just a gift, like many, from above, freely given through the Lord's love
Do we manage and plan the show, afraid not and a good thing too, you know?
Parental skills, never got right, passed from generation to generation in fright
How can one hope to get it sussed, when none before could claim such fuss

We but try and do our best, as those passed, sometimes in sleepless rest
Not knowing what is right to do, only hoping, praying, we'll see it through
From infant babe to child and adult come, survived, in-spite of Dad and Mum
Though we try our best in parental care - Thank God, He is always there!

21st June 2015

JUST A THOUGHT

We say; "I have a thought", was it something learnt, or something bought?
Was it distilled from earlier times via books and educated minds?
Maybe from time within the womb, forming subconscious, in watery flume
A sound of the external throng, musical notes on air, from bird song

Meaningful some, thoughts expressed, though certainly not always blessed
Just raw sharing a product of time, musings that are neither yours nor mine
Do we own these thoughts that come and go, drifting like flakes of snow?
Cannot grasp and hold them for long, melting quickly, in passing song

Inspiration, knowledge, reminders of what we knew, this we can't always do
Pass it on, while you can, others can sift out any nuggets from the pan
The bulk may be "pay dirt", gold miners say, for a shiny sparkler they pray
Sometimes cast upon the air, though others do not agree nor wish to share

Should they agree with what we think or say? tis only a thought for today
Tomorrow, another, quite different take, does not make today's muse a fake
Was just an insight, not too deep, I know what I mean, and this will keep?
It may be shared, though sometimes not, just a thought, soon forgot.

26th July 2015

STORMY WATERS

Clouds gather on horizon, not one alone, filling nicely with future foam
Gentle formation, yet, a distant stampeding herd, to ignore would be absurd
Distant dust, airborne on changing pressured air, soon it won't be Fair!
Gathering moisture from the deep, soon to deposit, in a mighty heap

Shining sun where we are, though signs of foreboding presence, not too far
Cries foretelling the coming, heard, on livening air flow, carrying bird
Setting for a sheltering spot, before the heaven dumps the lot
Wings now on turbo charge, gathering gloom is looming large

Craft we sail, sturdy and firm, ocean's might ignored at peril, we learn
Make preparations, vital we know, as much as possible stowed below
Ok storm come do your worst, a fine deluge to quench the thirst!
Stay calm; see it through, a blessed, skilful hand on tiller, for me and you

Down in torrents a wall of wet, storm force ten, not to forget
It is upon us without delay; "hold the line" the shout; "and pray"
We have been this course before, salted brine entering cabin door
Pump out excess, from bilges too, lend a hand, we shall get through!

Soon, as we saw before, it moves on by, shrieking wildly, looking for more
Chasing on, after slow start, leaving safe, soaked, crew, still full of heart
Such crises arise, come and go combinations of hail, winds, rain and snow
Best we can is all we do, as the Lord watches over to guide us through.

6th August 2015

PAST, PRESENT, FUTURE

Past times are gone, though not forgotten in this day, linking all we do and say
Weaving now, a thread of people thin, place and time, whence we did begin
Start, middle and end, a genetic composition we, influence of family tree?
Some we did not view, others we did know, some, only heard what they did do

Those, time afar, before we knew, how do they influence what we do?
Excuse not, for errors made, they are ours, no blaming ancient bones in grave!
Triumphs too, victorious joys, as young, middle, or aged girls and boys
Achievement, with others help and failure too, all in our package, me and you

Viewing onwards, the futures end, what is waiting around each bend?
We do not know, why should we try, tis enough to help each day go by
Tomorrow or even later today, is something for which we can, but pray
No wasting time, in concern of what to come, future is not ours, move on!

26th August 2015

COURAGE IN CONFUSION

Do we understand, what we say and do, is that me to me or me to you?
Confused, missing links, sometimes we send and take, oh for pity's sake!
No wonder we get misunderstood, stay true to self, it will be good
What is this ever-changing time, nothing new, just another rhyme?
Keep one on the straight and narrow, like plough share, scythe and harrow
Cultivate habit of peace and calm each day, helps to keep the woes away
Stay firm and focused not astray, for that ahead, we need not pray
This time we have, the ever present now, just to enjoy presently, and how
Peaceful, calm and slow forming thought, always best for learning taught
Sing songs of joy and praise, rocking with fun, for happy days
Lift the voice, your sound don't fear, all is sweetest music, in some ear
Express the feelings of the day, no matter how mysterious they are
They are your own for sharing, if you wish however, near or far
They can be accepted or rejected it doesn't matter now
For God understands where they come from and Loves you, anyhow!

30th October 2015

SPIRIT OF HOPE

Each day we are given, to start again, to live in hope, that we remain
In spite of trial and fun, tears and joy, seeing in all a chance to gain
Strength and spirit renewed each hour, the Spirit each does empower
To further strive and obtain, in spite of sadness, thirst, hunger and pain
Empowered by a new desire, to overcome, against what may conspire
A renewed Hope, not just a wish, a belief, through God's love, lost anguish
Continued steps along the way, guided, protected, come what may
A lighter touch, a springing step, once more renewed, Hopeful concept
No time for lengthy backward glance, tis onward now we focus and advance
Onwards and upwards, we know not how, faith and trust is needed now
Hope in the ever-loving God, as through all trials and joys, we daily trod
Sharing the mood, the thought, the anxious time, in Him, all hope is fine
A trust the like we cannot contrive, a faith in the One, with whom we thrive
An understanding, never to grasp, yet a Spirit of Hope, to always last.

15th November 2015

ADVENT JOURNEY

At this time of venturing forth, with yo ho ho, how far now have we to go?
Traversing life's challenges, valley and peak, remaining strong, not too weak
Time for reflection and for change, from wallet and from deeper range
To accept a gift, worth more than all, love from the Babe, within the stall

It's always there for those that want and those in need, tis true love, indeed
The Magi trio with their gifts came, had they nowt, His love the same
Good they were, to travel afar, following that bright heavenly star
Shining down to light the way, just as He does, for us each day

Light of the World shines constant and bright, for you and me, day and night
Though mine eyes, shadows see, He always clearly sees you and me
Onward in the daily life we go, through springtime rain or winter snow
Viewing the beauty, they present, just as those Wise men, Heaven sent

The shepherds too, angels they say, called them to the stable, on that day
Our Adventure continues now, the coming home we know not when, or how
Journey on with songs of joy, mirth and fun, as young girl and boy
The Hope that babe, brought in day of yore, is for us all, both rich and poor
Believe or not, His love is yours, even greater than that of Santa Claus
Onward we travel, light steps, we pray, to bring us to, His Christmas Day.

10th December 2015

BEING WHAT WE ARE

Expectations we have of others and self, book-filled dreams, leave on shelf
We are as we are today, why fighting to make it another way?
Imperfect yes, hoped, improving too, but knowing, as I am, WILL DO
Struggling to make it another way, may miss the opportunities of the day

To see the good and fun in others around, a bit of their treasure may be found
Looking more closely at their show, may reveal a view, of special inner glow
Helping to boost a flagging soul, lighting a pathway forward, with comment droll
The giver and recipient, both to gain, when being oneself and true, remain

Other's expectations, reasonable may be, but I am what I am, that is ME!
So, on we go, the you and me, passing by, only as others see
Externals viewed, is mostly what we see and hear, nothing of the inner fear
Be strong though, not on your own, we all have the One, so never alone!

Happy with what and how we are, see the inner gem that shines far
We all have a light to share, though maybe not always seen, in the glare
Listen, look, hear the sound, if deaf no matter, the Lords around
He never is, out of reach afar and He is happy to LOVE us as WE ARE.

13th December 2015

CHRISTMAS THOUGHTS

Here we are, counting down again, the Babe is coming, Santa at the rein
Cards being written, final posting day close by, seeing portents in the sky
Extra treats to fill the sack, letters to Santa, believe he's coming back!
Another year, that special day, listening out for bells, of church and sleigh

A special mix of holy joy, fun and laughter, prayer of girl and boy
Happiness of kind thought and word, a smile, a joke, enjoying the absurd
Is this unreal this joyous time, is it ok, is it really fine?
Of course, it is! it's Heaven sent, like all God's gifts, with love its meant

Year end approaches, another gone, joyous, brilliant, sad for some
A heady mix, life does provide, one thing's for sure, God is at our side
Those ups and downs, sadness and joy, His hope and strength, we employ
Accept the love of Creator being, overcoming problems now and unseen

Once again, we celebrate that birth, with prayerful thought and gentle mirth
Accepting the love, of God and Man, sharing, whatever gifts we can
Precious ones, cost not a penny, love, patience and fun, among the many
Received with joy, thanks and praise, Christmas Spirit, never fails to amaze.

20th December 2015

NEARLY THERE

Festivities continue, waning spirit maybe, fresh time coming for thee and me
Only hours now, till a brand-New Year and old 2015, does disappear
With it flys triumphs and tragedies too, many am sure both for me and you

Lessons learned, tasks achieved, a mix of writing and some pages leafed
Events multitudinous, large and small, each passing day, they did enthral
Some so joyous and mirth making too, some for others, not so to do

Tis what life, each year does bring, just as winter grips, before the spring
Not what happens, why or how, should we only deal with just the now?
After all, in time and place, we have no real power, just God's grace

To see us through, sadness and joy, that fighting Spirit to employ
Onwards and upwards, in good cheer, looking forward to, the coming year
Hope springs eternal and so it should, surely, without it, we be no good?

Man the ramparts, anchor weigh, full steam ahead and let us pray
For the strength and love, time ahead requires, making use of all the hours
Enjoying the gifts we have to share, lifting spirits of those, in burdened care

No matter how clever, smart or dim we are, we can follow that guiding star
Differing paths, though journeying same, via city street or country lane
On a helping hand, we all rely, to smile, going forward, as we try

May new days coming, special and fun, be filled with joyful hope of the Son.

29th December 2015

2016

FED UP

"I am fed up" I hear you say, so am I, another day
"What is fed up?" I ask myself, have I eaten all upon the shelf?
This; "fed", of which we say we feel, is it oh so very real?

Cannot find the; "fed" of which we speak, where is it, that I try to seek?
Is it up or is it down, how does it create a frown?
I say it's up, that fed you know, so why if fed up, feeling low?

A conundrum yes it surely is, a load of rubbish like some quiz
A poor description, less maybe, than how one feels, in reality
No wonder one does get confused, when looking at the language used

One might as well say; "Up Fed, I am feeling today"
Ah, that sounds a positive start, as; "Up with the lark" and Fed well too!
Could it be that, low feelings expressed in reverse, help one get over the worse

To lift one's thoughts to higher things, as lark ascending on the wing
The warmth of love and life and time, free for all, both yours and mine
With spirits raised, thought focussed high, once more reaching, to the sky

Expressed feelings of the now, better place oneself for future how
With "fed up" or "up fed" cast aside, once more go forward, stride by stride
Singing songs, maybe not in key, doesn't matter for you and me
A lightened heart, in many a way, will get us through each, God given day.

23rd January 2016

HOME AT LAST

A mighty journey Al, that voyage these past weeks, you did take
And now you have arrived on God's own shore, to live in peace for evermore
A constant watch, Chris and loving crew did keep, as you, bravely, traversed the deep

Loving thoughts, greater than words can express, always for you, nothing less
Prayers a plenty pouring forth, to help ease your passage going forth
Now in Heaven, no longer aboard, rejoicing, at peace, with the Lord

Candles burn, our prayers still heard, though we no longer hear your word
Action now, will be sent, by the sister, I lovingly know as, AL the Eloquent
You will, forever, be still active in our lives, those examples of love and counsel wise

We'll keep in touch in prayer and thought, sharing a laugh, re bargain bought!
You will be listening and watching o'er, as we sail on life's passage, just offshore
When life's storms arise and winds do gust, your example to us, will be a must

To cling in faith to love of God and Man, doing all we reasonably can
To bring hope and joy to those we meet, just as you did, in home and street
So, Al, until we meet again, in that Heavenly home, we will not be morose nor alone

You will be busy there, lovingly caring, for Skipper Chris and family crew, while not forgetting, young brother Joe too!

REST IN PEACE AL   Love Always XX
25 February 2016

CYCLE OF LIFE

Funny old thing, this cycle of life, from start to finish, without respite
Onwards it goes, sleep through to wake, dawn to dusk, here it does take
Doesn't stop there, it's just a start, depart this world, eternal life imparts
How lucky we are, to come this way, a journey to undertake each day
A gift of travelling many a path, sharing joy and sadness, with a laugh
Life ongoing, now Heaven beckons, better indeed, changing gear, to God speed
Attacking hills with vigour, as we ride, courage of the Lord, deep inside
Steering life's many a crooked path, avoiding potholes and their wrath
Changing through gears, older we grow, lighter the peddling, as we slow
Yet onward and upwards, enjoying the view, in hope and trust, coming through
Soon enough approach the final bend, assured a joyous welcome, for God's friend.

15th March 2016

EASTER THOUGHTS

Tis time for eggs au chocola, to celebrate His rising star
The One who gave His life to save, our eternity, beyond the grave
Remembering, suffering endured, in human frailty, though still the Lord
Pain and loss, just as we, yet final compassion on that tree
Human pain and loss, He did endure, for our salvation, now and evermore
Family and friends, gathered round, as broken bones, lowered, to the ground
A cave for grave, tis said it was, a shelter, hiding such great loss
Mother and friends, after Sabbath came, finding, only, cloths remain
God made Man, as promised, risen, overcoming death's, stark prison
Pointing Salvation's way, to us all, no longer stymied, by the Fall
Saving all, then, now and those gone before, the gift of Life, forever more
So let this joyous memorial feast, forever be, a life of Hope, for you and me

24th March 2016 (Holy Thursday)

SPRING

The rain falls, the winds blow, the clouds are low - is Spring here?
Sodden ground, stilled bird sound, water all around - is Spring here?
Heating on, winter clothes not yet gone - is Spring here?
Gloomy skys' above, bare branches cold still hold - is Spring here?
Wait, a song thrush starting to sing, could it be the ring - that Spring is here?
In spite of the falling rain, life is starting again - I wonder is Spring here?
Shake off the winter break, come alive, awake - yes, surely Spring is near?
Time to start anew, the darkness, come through - yes, Spring maybe here
New hope for clearing skys, a warmth to dry the eyes - could Spring be here?
New challenge and joy each day, will help us on our way - when Spring is here
"In due season", say, is what we have today - enjoy now, YES Spring is here!

2nd April 2016

ARISE AT DAWN

A new day awakes, from slumber it takes, to start an adventure or two
Mind now alert, time to act while still pert and strike out to admire the view
But before, tea and toast, with Lady Bloss most, in Snug, a moment or 2

Window view admire, thoughts tend to conspire, with plans for me and you
Sunshine or rain we are off up lane, opening Lord's house for the day
Then a meadow meander, plus a gander, at what remains of night's prey

Tufts of fur, feathers scattered, badger, scratched dung holes, we spy
Fox demised by gate, oh tis too late, should be quicker when out on hunt
If he expected lamb served with ham on a plate, sorry not for this old mate!

Buzzards and crows, to feast well I suppose, on a very fine meal today
Broods delighted with food with such ease, plus Foxy's multi vitamin fleas
Rabbits now large, see Lady Bloss and depart, no doesn't decide to chase

A pheasant calling, springing more appealing this morning, than a hot race
As sporting activities draw to a close, no mushrooms spotted today
A dip in the trough, gentle waters cooling off, then home- Day is under way!

18th July 2016

LET THEM BE

If they disagree, with what you know, let them be
If they annoy and frustrate, let them be
If they increasingly, agitate, let them be
If they show no empathy or understanding, let them be
If they are fixed in view and unrelenting in their passion, let them be
If their political colour is not of yours, let them be
If their social strata differs from your own, let them be
If their Faith, or None, fails coincide with yours, let them be
If they are of superior intelligence or wisdom, let them be
If their gender, race, nationality, or religion, differs from yours, let them be
If you are fortunate, they too, will let YOU BE!

1st August 2016

BANK HOLIDAY

Time to relax, escape the drudge, for those employed - do not begrudge!
No matter what the weather be, time to enjoy, late summer revelry
What ere it is, you choose today, in city, dancing or country harvest eh?
A seaside stay, under sail or beach, the choice is yours, if in reach

Carnival music, many hear, to herald beauty, foreclosing summer year
Bands, parades, roads amassed, with travellers getting nowhere fast
Some fly ore skys' to get away, not returning till another day
Whatever path you choose to take, enjoy it for its own sake

The gift of holi / holy days, be they Bank or Sun, whatever sways
To be enjoyed, as much as can, refreshment for life's extended span
Forget the cares and even woe, do not let them spoil it, just let them go
This day, our only gift of now, enjoy, revitalised, in hope another be allowed.

29th August 2016

CREATIVITY

Let words and thoughts flow, no matter how fast, or slow
Creative they may be, or blank as paper sheet
A thought is YOURS, owned by only you, a word may be shared, if wanted to
How are formed, amaze to think, some when sleeping, or at kitchen sink

Creativity just comes and goes, as the disappearing, thawing, snows
Words spoken, sink beneath the wave, a few lasting beyond the grave
Conjoined, now and then, future thought and times, we know not when
Does not matter, no need to plan, let them flow, when ere you can

Moved to create or be inspired, through words or song however fired
Burnished with the freedom of thought, oft more helpful, than book bought
Communication relying, on the listening, as much as spoken words
Absorbing the essentials and kicking out the absurd

The thoughts and words, processing long, many also now in song
Along they go each and every day, accompanying us on our way
Some, not easily understood, some, best forgot, some, though not
By whatever means, they come or go, they may have be good to know!

3rd September 2016

CONVICTIONS

They are held firm, they are held close, to some they are the very most
The thing to cling to, day to day, steadfast still, what ere others say
Integral to one's being, thought and self, always there upon the shelf
Occasionally lifted and dusted down, the gloss restored, straightened crown

Some are, happily, with others shared, others only bring, unhappy, glares
Whatever response, tis still the same, they are yours, held without shame
Respecting others right to hold, diametrically opposed to yours of old
Eclectic mix, like we today, develop and comprise, what we think and say

Strong or not, even weakly held, they are the essence of our weld
The glue, holding intact our being, always present yet unseen
To deny them, weakens what we are, though to amend, can lift the bar
To higher climes, of thought and deed, with firm, living, conviction we succeed

17th September 2016

THERE IS A TIME

There is a time and a place, to grasp the nettle (gloves optional), set the pace
It comes upon us, when we wake, each to be sure, make no mistake
The chance to grow, the chance to learn, options abound, steel in furnace burn

Brandish the sword with vigour and strength, stepping forward, stride of length
Not to trample those in path, nor even slay their dragon, as we pass
But moving forward, steadfast each day, onward, steady, with a little pray

Not too sanctimonious, as we go, feet on the ground, no wings yet to show
Opportunities each day brings, to start anew, on many things
Dealing with the now, as best we can, caring for our fellow Man
To raise a smile of joy, with ditty rhyme, maybe now, is that Time!

27th September 2016

MOMENTS

A moment's joy, a tuneful lyre, the great outdoors, the hearth and fire
All of these, in their own way, lead some to tranquillity, for which they pray
A boisterous jape, a spot of wine, joyous time to pass, tween boy and lass
A silent place, of momentous calm, but for the breeze and feathered alarm
A deafening silence this can be, while scurrying in the undergrowth, a frenzy
All quiet once again, to some turmoil, to another, undergone in pain
Away from despair and worry fraught, the things lost, or should have brought
Always remember in time of care, peace, hope and joy prevail somewhere
Arriving back, equilibrium found, feet now firmly on the ground
A place and space, of peace and calm, amidst a world full of alarm
A surprising location it may be, in City Street or under a tree
Allowing mind and heart and soul, to open up, unfurl a mighty scroll
Accepting all that life provides, helping one to grow, a little, inside.

8th October 2016

EACH DAY

From slumbers now awaken, new dawn has come, fresh horizons beckon
Opportunities, with commencing day, to love, to live, to do and pray
Explore horizons, maybe few; nonetheless, they are there for us to view
Tread forth, slow or swift, does not matter what, the speed or the drift

Potential for some bright new thought or plan, always there, for everyone
Seizing the moment, as it presents, prospects bright, in every sense
A challenge met, achieved or not, t'was moment seized, nay to be forgot
Outcomes fade, in significance, as further opportunities advance

On sad or times of woe, why dwell? Opportunities now this day foretell
Newly presented, refreshed, renewed, twenty-four hours a day exudes
Not to miss, what it has to say, forgetting about a future way
Maximising all this one presents, each and every one, of its events

Not always easy, staying the course, ups and downs and sometimes worse
Each day, a heady mix, of challenges and joys, some we cannot fix
No matter what presents at time, what comes to us, is yours and mine
Embrace it now, as best we can, this way, it's the only one we have today.

17th October 2016

THE FUTURE

Why anticipate the future, who knows what it may bring?
A sleepless night, a sunny day, or some enjoyable thing
Detailed planning for when, is surely that of God, not Men
It may come and it may go, only time will tell, is all we know

When anticipation is bright, all is well, when dark, a living hell
Assessment of what is to come, may cloud the now, and then miss some
This moment now, is all we own, making the most before lain prone
Tis a gift, to joyfully share, with all of those for whom we care

Time not to be wasted on future fear, that like as not, will never appear
And if it does, come what may; be strengthened by this present day
A lot to gain, a lot to bring, to receive and give, almost everything
The now we have, to enjoy and do, what is best for me and you

26th October 2016

A MOMENT

Wondering what it is, or where it went, may not have been, nor time spent
A thought, a word, or fine something, tis come and gone, just as the spring
To chase it now would be in vain, as chasing rabbits down a lane
They are gone now, and so is it, that missing note a stupid twit!

Scant reminder of something new or past, a fleeting moment, gone too fast
Off it goes, in chariot fine, drawn by pantomime horses, six mice, fine
Far flung the future, past and present be, just stay a moment now and see
A moment, still, this now we have, resting, quiet, joyous or sad

A time to stay, for what it's worth we know not, it is here now and not forgot
Hectic, dashing round has stopped, brief thoughts, a ha, the penny dropped
Oh yes I see, it all makes sense, needed time to rebuild, the broken fence
The one that divides the fog from clear, it's in the head between the ear

Do not ponder it too, for very long, that moment, in either verse or song
Letting it come and then to go, is the secret to accepting, that I know
Dealing with what it leaves tis true, poses a challenge for me and you
Needless stress, thinking it through, tis gone, as come, from out the blue.

7th November 2016

LEST WE FORGET

Remembrance yes, a solemn time, though, not bringing back, lives so fine
Lost in futility of war, on this land and foreign shore
A tragedy in every case, an abomination, of the human race
Lacking ability to walk together, ensuring many, separated forever

Politicians are not just to blame; each allowed to do it, in our name
They cannot monger all alone, just encouraged onwards, by our own
"Horror", yes, we do proclaim, as they play that waging card again
Yet, we convince ourselves, the War is; "just", a fight to have, is a "must"

Now is the time, to remember how they went, young lives needlessly spent
And still they are sent, this very hour, on missions glorified, for political power
A politics of peace, one day may come, worth praying for, by everyone
A hope, a wish, little cost, negating need, for remembrance, of further loss.

13th November 2016

CHRISTMAS CONTENTMENT

It comes at times, to one and all, in varying bursts both large and small
To young and old, a special sense, of more too life, than just makes sense
A peace, a joy, so splendid aye, momentarily with us, from on high
Sometimes it stays for moments, hours, or days, or just suddenly always

What ere time it takes, tis of it's own, just maybe shows, we are not alone
"Time is no man's", a saying goes, onward to summer sun, as winter snows
The time of year does not affect the peace and splendour it can reflect
Moments of inner peace and warmth maybe, just a gift for thee and me

So now when it comes, as sure it will, enjoy those moments to the full
From whence and how, tis a surprise, no one sees through God's eyes!
So don't fret too much, just a little maybe, about the pressies and the tree
Relax, at least a brief moment, allowing space for Christmas Contentment.

20th December 2016

THE POLITICAL INCORRECTNESS

Grandiose ideas, oft old and revamped, to allay our fears
Leading on to better times, a familiar political clarion chimes
A scheme to better all schemes past, this one will work, at last!

Marvellous, how great you are, now let me see, will it go far?
Oh, I think we saw this all before, under another colour, I am sure
Just a revamp this, wait and see, the last one failed for you and me

Go away and think again, this politics is just a game
The pawns it seems elect the few, who screw it up again, anew
And so it goes, select the fools, who conjure up the rules

To make our land a better place, those leaders of the human race
Great nations, to which all aspire, just like the long-fallen Empire
Roman, British, off they went, collapsing into many a fragment

A political view, narrow of mind, guided only by a latest find
Civil Servant striving hard, hoists Minister on his own petard
A brief one-off gain, or loss, not needed now, who gives a toss?

Plebs need us keeping them from self harm, do not understand our charm
Our selfless actions for their good, bit like the legendary Robin Hood
One day as Election draws near, we will promise to remove their every fear

We are correct, we must be so, those Plebs elected us you know
No Party mantra, follow we, just solid independent thinkers working for thee
Please don't be cynical, you see, we are Correct, you can believe in me!

30th December 2016

2017

THOUGH DIVIDED, TOGETHER WE STAND

Separate, in so many ways, some by years, others only by days
Age and race bring division too, religion also, in a separate pew
Objection, agreement, a divisive word, coming together, makes it absurd
Healthy and sick, support both need, divided resources, both to feed

A weakness or strength, will sometimes be, less divisive, than we may see
The black, the white, the pink, the blue, all coming together for me and you
A difference yes, no wrong in that, supporting all, in strength, a fact!
Individuals we, separately, God made, an agnostic, believer, atheist, braid

Division and union, in the plan, not easily perceived, nor understood by Man
The coming and going, in opposite ways, can this lead to halcyon days?
Maybe it can, if some turnaround and listen to something, of others sound
"Join us", or "can we you", is all need be said, try it now, before dead!

It doesn't take many; others stop and stand, soon now, a gathering grand
Though opposite tides, parallel go, slowing a little, forming circular flow
An increasing depth, of human good will, smoothing out, the divisive chill
Individual, separate, even the grand, though still divided, together we stand.

15th January 2017

ALLEGIANCE

It has a value, to be sure, strength in togetherness, not to ignore
Can be heartfelt too, strong from within or only floating, as a whim
Solid, strong, conviction aye, or maybe, passing phase of inward eye
Whatever kind it may be, it can be effective, for thee and me

But consequence of strong held belief, does not always bring relief
From rights and wrongs, experienced now, or in the past, no matter how
Changing times and values too, not all wrong, though oft misconstrued
Not wrong, this passionate belief, still allowing space, for other's relief

Allegiance, Conviction, Faith and Hope, conjoined by Atheist and Pope
Family, nation or humankind, a sense of belonging and support may find
Blurring, logical processed thought, too easily leads to chaos wrought
Stick together, come what may, call of despots, tyrants and we that pray

Not as simple as we think, to meld black and white with blue and pink
As we our favourite leanings keep, respect of the other, may help sleep
Retaining loyalty, as inclined, will too, assist the peace of mind
Allegiance yes, in its place Good, so too Division, both gifts from Above

22nd January 2017

THOUGHTS POLITICO

It polarises worlds and debate, people's hearts, still love and hate
Encompasses minds, hearts and lives a many, those with or not a penny
Some trying to change the world, some themselves, others just to delve
Mighty plans, lowly ones too, to make improvement for me and you
Or so they would have you believe, tis never them who do deceive!

A moral high ground of right and wrong; "we know best" is their song
But who is to blame for such things? why, you and me they do sing
In unison, with one voice too, the ones to blame are me and you
We do, after all, put them there, with gifted votes of those who care
To influence outcome, making a better lot, than the one currently got

Tis no wonder then that things go wrong, as we all sing a different song
Left and right, middle too, we, none of us, really have a clue
Words expressed and media hype, a game played by particular type
Lofty thought and expression gave, the call for millions to an early grave
Moral high ground, in battle fields lay, the politician's debris, bones array

Not just in war they lead us, dying in our streets today -starvation plus!
Pain and suffering of a different kind, some of body, some of mind
Hopelessness felt, at their lot, some self-inflicted, other by politic clot
Decisions affecting all involved, those personal and joint, are manifold
Some good, some bad, even nondescript, all impact on, where we fit

A grain of selfishness is here, as at the political wanderers, I sneer
Involvement, is one way of course, or, let them bring water to the horse
If the latter course we take, beware the possibility, they make a mistake
The pure and clear aqua filled trough, may contain some dodgy stuff
By accident or, even design, the gifted liquid may not be so fine!

Whatever times in which we live, days now or past, learnt politics give
Same old ways to do the job, no new thoughts, as yet, put on the hob
Politico pot, mixing right and left, cosmopolitan brew, always bereft
Of truly fine and nourishing food, sustaining each and every brood
Awaiting new way to be found, until then, by current flaws, we be bound.

11th February 2017

HELP YOURSELF

Helping hand so very good and kind, self-help even finer, one may find
While still time, rely not on other Man, but on the gifts possessed, still fine
Used wisely, not wasted on a whim, they still keep burning, tho maybe thin
While they still have a life and glow, let them continue to help you grow

A time will come when they start to dim, till then, let them create a din
No cry for help, that's premature, garner what you have and use it for sure
Onward, use of your own resource, supporting arm only for brief recourse
Strive to serve yourself and others too, all have a continuous thing to do

Slipping, sliding or stumbling along, tis chance for appropriate song
Joyous, melancholy loud or soft, all to be used for to lifting oneself aloft
On others tho we may rely, helping ourselves, must always try
Whatever time or place foresee, special joy of helping self, will always be.

13th February 2017

HEAR THE MUSIC

Hear the chant, plain mellow sound, in it for some, peace found
A rousing chorus doth too prevail, to lift away the cobwebbed veil
A Reggae verse, deep meaning too, all inspired for me and you

Every taste satisfied, in tune found, somewhere deep in musical sound
A mood lifted, a thought expressed, whatever way, it's composer's best
Inspired notation, whence we no not, some of distant melodies forgot

All unique in their own way, yet continuous message still holds sway
The inward spirit, let gleam forth, by notational inspiration wrought
Movement of the heart and soul, via Gregorian chant plus Rock and Roll

Whatever musical taste maybe, singular or eclectic, let it be free
Enjoy the inspired sound, lifting despaired up from off the ground
Spirits revived, for some to hold, where words of comfort are too cold

Notation diverse, every sound all meaningful, by another found
And so the power of music brings, to those who listen or just sing
Those too, that instruments do play, receive inspiration on that day.

2nd March 2017

POSITIVE THOUGHT

With a positive thought or two, just see, what it can do, for me and you
For others too, some help may bring, a forward step along, this Spring
May not take all cares away, could help some get most, out of the day
A cloud may darken, just awhile, tho positive thought, could raise a smile

Won't solve all problems in this way, yet lighten burdens, it may
Not only you, this may lift, for others too, a needed gift
Starting with a smile or two, the face to crack and laugh breaks through
To lighten life and fine some joy, is surely good for girl and boy

The negative, too easily seen, time to blur it's darkening beam
Let positive ray of light shine through, a little help for me and you
So much we have, for sure to thank, no exploding shells from other's tank
A light and living life of Spring, so much happiness, we still can bring.

1st April 2017

WHAT TO MAKE OF IT ALL?

So what to make of it all, whether young or old, big or small?
To fathom it out, not easy that, too complicated, like singing flat!
It doesn't resonate too well, whether becalmed, or in the swell
Fish are caught and goals scored, yet thoughts, sometimes, best ignored
Stay the course, we tend to say, just to take it, day by day
Of course, this is the best to do, tis the only option for me and you!
Can't deal with tomorrow or yesterday past, the now is even fading fast
So make what you can, while it's within your gift, maybe, give others a lift
They too, may make something of their fate, with a hand from a mate
Lifting one up when they fall, may help us, make something of it All!

29th May 2017

VIEWPOINT

Whatever it may be, the view one holds, is your validity
Does not always have a share, with others who, equally care
The viewpoint, whatever it may strive, formulated in a different narrative
A meeting of minds, rarely achieved, tis good too, airing thoughtful seed

Growth, always needed to sustain and avoid, stagnating, cerebral pain
Thought and silent contemplate, also enhance, future, lively debate
Formulation of a view, may challenge many, or a few
Tis a God given freedom, to inspire, enabling all, to further enquire

Other viewpoint, audacious though it seem, receive with open glean
Non judgemental appraisal see, allowing understanding, if not agree
The other view, in conscientious hold, valued to the owner, just as gold
A review, in light of wisdom, insight too, fed each viewpoint, as it grew.

2nd July 2017

THE FUTURE

The future I know not, nor do I care
Why should I? for it will be of itself out there
To fear it is useless, to welcome it, impossible
To share in it, also a task unreal

Whatever it be, for thee or me
Be sure, a surprise, it will have on board
If only the same, as before, it bring, 'twill be some change from today's known thing

No certainty here, as in yesteryear, or maybe it wasn't so then?
For, sure footedness gone, still to walk on, not foreseen this, a way to tread
The seasons they come, and they go, with slight alteration of course
Equinox shadows now traverse, daylight hour, increased or reversed

Whatever time of life, place name, or date, maybe you have enough on your plate
Could your platter is larger than you think, as too, the wash bowl in the sink?

In which case, the contents won't fall off the edge, even now room, for more to wedge
Our communal platter gets filled and emptied each day, a lot for some for others nay

The fulsome, wholeness, of today, not guaranteed, enjoy while you can, it may take leave
If it goes, no longer there, you shared in it, sometime, somewhere

Understanding of things great or small, not guaranteed, forever, to recall
Even that, is not the end, for many a surprise, awaits round every bend
Opportunities beckon, all life through, so take them, at ebb and flood, too

3rd September 2017

AS UNDERSTANDING FADES

To understand what does it mean? to many knowledge, or cognitive skill
For others, to assimilate with empathy and demonstrate no ill
Not easy this, whatever state in life, "facio cognosco", of confused strife
The leaving of the previous state, moving on to Heavenly Gate

Meanwhile, strive, hold on to what we've got, for that is a lot
Try open new paths and synaptic links, old may go, so new ones think
No boundaries there you see, no possibility too great, for me
Opportunity each day, to be; "taken at the flood", as the Bard did say.

Comprehension of what we do and say, hard to assimilate each day
No rhyme nor reason, many a time, no comprehension, just me / mine
How can others comprehend, when you cannot a clear message send
Of first import, You know what You think, later, may only be a blink

So, tis time now, to continue anew, for however long or few
The hours and days provided now, to build an understanding of how
To construct, a further, cunning plan, to assist oneself and fellow Man
Conventional ways, gradually fade, You are always the You, God made!

11th October 2017

HELP YOURSELF

You have the gifts, both great and small, so go make the best of all!
Hopes, visions, dreams and woes, God grants ability, to meet all those
Don't wait for others, they have their issues too; give it a go, just You
While you can, take the rein, use your strengths and remaining brain

Surprise yourself and others too, there is still plenty more to do
Move things along, each day a gain, achievement / loss, none in vain
Another step along the way, come rain or shine, still make the hay
Harvest yield, plenty gathered, to feed the soul and life untethered.

22nd October 2017

Thank you Joe for sharing your thoughts with your family and friends.

Lightning Source UK Ltd.
Milton Keynes UK
UKHW010645060820
367788UK00001B/7